W9-DEC-127

609
Nea

Neal, Harry Edward
From Spinning Wheel to
Spacecraft

DATE DUE

From Spinning Wheel to Spacecraft

The Story of The Industrial Revolution

The fascinating story of how modern man made the swift ascent from an age dominated by drudgery and superstition to the life of comparative comfort and sophistication that we know today. It tells how bold and gifted men invented machines and made startling discoveries that changed the manners, morals and standards of living all over the world—all in the span of two centuries. Woven through this account are the individual stories of inventors and scientists who braved ridicule, poverty and often violence to bring their discoveries to the world. Highlighting the events of what has come to be known as the Industrial Revolution, the author points to the fact that today we are undergoing still another industrial revolution, and the changes that result may be as great as those that have already occurred.

Books by Harry Edward Neal

Informational

THE TELESCOPE

SIX AGAINST CRIME
Treasury Agencies in Action

COMMUNICATION
From Stone Age to Space Age

TREASURES BY THE MILLIONS
The Story of The Smithsonian Institution

DIARY OF DEMOCRACY
The Story of Political Parties in America

FROM SPINNING WHEEL TO SPACECRAFT
The Story of The Industrial Revolution

THE MYSTERY OF TIME

Career

NATURE'S GUARDIANS
Your Career in Conservation

PATHFINDERS, U.S.A.
Your Career on Land, Sea and Air

SKYBLAZERS
Your Career in Aviation

DISEASE DETECTIVES
Your Career in Medical Research

ENGINEERS UNLIMITED
Your Career in Engineering

MONEY MASTERS
Your Career in Banking

YOUR CAREER IN ELECTRONICS

YOUR CAREER IN FOREIGN SERVICE

From
Spinning Wheel
to
Spacecraft

The Story of The Industrial Revolution

by HARRY EDWARD NEAL

Illustrated with photographs

JULIAN MESSNER
NEW YORK

Published simultaneously in the United States
and Canada by Julian Messner, a division of
Simon & Schuster, Inc.,
1 West 39 Street, New York, N.Y. 10018.
All rights reserved.

Fifth Printing, 1967

We are grateful to the following for the use of their
photographs: American Telephone & Telegraph Co.,
Argonne National Laboratory, Association of Amer-
ican Railroads, Atomic Energy Commission, Ford
Motor Company, General Dynamics Corporation,
Goodyear Tire & Rubber Co., Gulf Oil Corporation,
Library of Congress, National Association of Manu-
facturers, Old Slater Mill Museum, Philadelphia Col-
lege of Textiles & Science, Philip Lesly Company,
Radio Corporation of America, Remington Rand,
Smithsonian Institution, Southern Railway Company,
States Marine Lines, U.S. Department of Agriculture.

Printed in the United States of America

Library of Congress Catalog Card No. 64–11814

Acknowledgments

For helpful information or photographs (or both, in some cases) I am deeply indebted to Bernard C. Harter of the News Service Branch of the U. S. Atomic Energy Commission; T. D. Geoghegan, Assistant Director of Public Relations, U. S. Steel Corporation, Washington, D. C.; Mrs. M. G. Hoffman, Standard Oil Company of New Jersey, Washington, D.C.; Henry R. Lamar, Assistant Director of Public Information, National Association of Manufacturers, New York; William H. Bunce, Special Representative, Association of American Railroads, Washington; Paul H. Oehser, Chief of the Editorial and Publications Division of The Smithsonian Institution, Washington; Jack Gertz, News Service Supervisor of The American Telephone & Telegraph Company, Washington; Ted Silvey of the AFL-CIO, Washington; Stanley K. Graham, Educational Services Coordinator, Ford Motor Company, Dearborn, Mich.; Paul Campbell, Historian, The Goodyear Tire & Rubber Co., Akron, Ohio; James B. Ellis, American Textile Manufacturers Institute, Inc., Charlotte, N. C.; Bruce E. Strasser, Head, Technical Information

Department, Bell Telephone Laboratories, New York; W. H.
Fortenberry, Assistant Chief of the Cotton Division, Standards
and Testing Branch, Agricultural Marketing Service, U. S.
Department of Agriculture; Mrs. John V. Hodgkins, Secretary of the Old Slater Mill Museum, Pawtucket, R. I.; A. A.
Gioia, Public Relations Department, Gulf Oil Corp., Pittsburgh, Pa.; Sidney M. Robards, Director of Public Relations
for the Radio Corporation of America, New York; and E. A.
Stromberg, Special Assistant to the Federal Highway Ad-
ministrator, Bureau of Public Roads, U. S. Department of
Commerce, Washington.

I am especially grateful to Miss Crimora Waite, Librarian
of the Culpeper County (Va.) Library, for her kindness and
help in obtaining much useful reference material for me from
the Culpeper Library and also from the Virginia State Library
in Richmond.

Harry Edward Neal

Introduction

One day years ago, when I was a boy in grammar school in Pittsfield, Massachusetts, the schools closed for the afternoon, a happy event for us kids. Better yet, the *reason* for the closing gave us one of the greatest thrills of our young lives. An airplane (we called it "air-e-o-plane") was to fly over our town for everyone to see.

I suppose I was then about seven or eight. Planes were few, and when one finally got to Pittsfield for the first time it was a big event. The ship, a biplane, flew high and low and zigged and zagged so that everybody in town had a chance to get a good look at it.

Today huge aircraft of many kinds zip through the skies over Pittsfield, and few folks, if any, even look up.

I can also remember a boyhood friend, Ray Tanner, who built a tiny crystal radio set in the days when "radio" was a new word in our language. At his invitation one night I shared a pair of earphones with him and listened to faint sounds of music and an occasional voice, but the sounds were obscured by noises like squeals and the crunching of cornflakes. Ray told me that the music was coming from an orchestra playing at the General Electric Company in Schenectady, New York.

When I went home and told my grandmother about the marvelous invention, she laughed. I don't remember her exact words, but they were something like: "Who ever heard of such foolishness? Lands sakes alive, why do you believe everything you're told? Now you get along to bed. Scoot!"

Grandmother didn't live long enough to hear a radio broadcast, although she did learn about radio from the newspapers.

As a youngster, seeing my first airplane and listening to my first radio program, I wasn't aware that I was seeing and hearing a part of what we now call the Industrial Revolution. Today other children are watching televised pictures of astronauts being rocketed into orbit around the earth, or "live" pictures of goings-on in faraway lands, beamed into our homes by way of a communications satellite in space. Schools are teaching students how to operate electronic computers which can do complex work in seconds that might take many men days, weeks or months to do. These young people are seeing and taking part in a new Industrial Revolution although, like me, they may not be aware of it in these terms.

In the pages ahead I have tried to tell about the important inventions and the people who have brought us to this stage of history. In so doing I have learned that in many respects history repeats itself and that man sometimes fails to learn by lessons of the past.

I also discovered that some historians play fast and loose with facts. For example, I found three different sources giving three different times for the launching of Robert Fulton's steamboat, the *Clermont*. Worse yet, I found one source that identified an inventor as a sailor from a famous family in

Nantucket, Massachusetts, when in fact he was from Baltimore, Maryland, and not a sailor at all!

With the records available to me I have tried to be as accurate as possible. There may be discrepancies in dates or statistics between my work and the works of others, but an author has to be selective and make his own judgments based on the whole of his research. It is *what* happened and not especially *when* it happened that is important.

Harry Edward Neal

Contents

CHAPTER 1

Do It Yourself—Or Forget It

In 1725, in the back country of western Massachusetts, a tall slender youth named Jonathan fell in love with a beautiful red-haired girl named Molly, the daughter of a stern, hardworking farmer. Jonathan asked Molly to be his wife.

"Oh, yes, Jonathan, yes!" Molly exclaimed. They kissed, and Molly laughed. "I was afraid you wouldn't ask me. Go quickly, now, and get my father's consent."

Jonathan's smile faded and he looked as though he had been ordered to enter a cage of hungry bears.

"What's the matter?" Molly asked.

"Your father is—uh—well, it ain't easy to talk to him."

Molly nodded. "I know. But you must." She patted his arm and added, "Don't worry. He wants me to wed. He knows you've been courtin' me. He'll be expectin' you to ask."

"You coming with me?"

"Oh, no, Jonathan. 'Twouldn't be right and fittin'. Go on, now. He's in the barn. I'll wait right here."

So Jonathan ambled slowly toward the barn, trying to

13

think of what he would say. He picked up a stick, took a jackknife from his pocket and began to whittle. Whittling helped to steady his nerves, and if he whittled while he talked with Molly's father he wouldn't have to look constantly into the old man's penetrating dark eyes.

The farmer was mending a broken wagon wheel when Jonathan approached him. "Mornin'," Jonathan said.

"Mornin'."

"Looks like rain, mebbe," Jonathan said.

"Mebbe." The old man went on with his work and Jonathan kept at his whittling. Long thin shavings were cut off the stick and fell curling to the floor until finally the old man stopped his work, wiped his face with his shirt sleeve and said, "Want somep'n, boy?"

Jonathan whittled faster and stammered, and with only a shy glance or two at the older man he managed to say, "I come to ask for Molly's hand in wedlock."

The farmer didn't answer for what seemed a long time. He simply watched Jonathan's stick being reduced swiftly and almost completely to a pile of shavings on the barn floor. "Jonathan," the farmer said, "you're a good-enough looker, I find no fault with your talk, I like your Paw and Maw, and I know you'll come into property someday."

A wonderful feeling of relief flooded upward from Jonathan's toes. Then Molly's father went on, "But you can't marry up with Molly."

Jonathan's mouth came open, and he dropped what was left of the stick. "But—but—" he said, shaking his head slowly.

The farmer picked up the small stub of whittled stick. "See that? What is it?"

"Just a piece of wood," Jonathan answered, more puzzled than ever.

"Yep. Just a piece of wood. Now, then—if you had made somethin' *useful* out of this piece of wood when you were doin' all that whittlin', if you had made an arrow, a wedge, a plug, or almost anything out of it instead of just cuttin' away, you could have Molly. But you didn't, and you can't."

Jonathan tried to smile. "You're joshin' me. I don't see—"

"I ain't joshin' you, son. The point is that if you work and waste you'll likely live and waste, too. When you come into your property you'll whittle it away like you did the stick, and afore you know it you won't have nothin' left, and my Molly would go hungry, mebbe even barefoot." He handed the stick to Jonathan and went back to mending the wagon wheel.

The records do not reveal whether Jonathan and Molly ever married. There are many records, however, that do show how vitally important it was for pioneer men and women to avoid wasting talent, time and raw materials. In his book, *The Great Inventions*, F. B. Wilkie wrote:

The farmer could no more get along without his jackknife than he could without his plow or animals for draught. It is in demand a score of times every day; it labors when its owner labors and rests only when he sleeps. If the whiffletree band becomes loose it is the jackknife which furnishes the wedge and the remedy. It provides a plug for the leaky washtub or the barrel of vinegar; it . . . shapes the shingle into a spoon with which the boy applies ashes to the young and growing corn. It . . . reduces the dimensions of the new helve for the ax, and supplies the wedges with which it is held in place. It furnishes the missing pegs for the warping bars, the sticks for the complaining swifts; hollows the boat and slices the finger of the boy as he labors to secure a craft for the goose pond or the creek. . . . It cuts the young hemlock or the branch of hickory which is destined for the bow, and prepares the arrows with their notched ends to fit the string. . . . It makes huge yawning chasms in the pine of the school desk, gouges holes through the seats, slices slivers from the slate-frame and decorates the adjacent fences with notches, hollows, and all species of figures in bas and alto relief. . . .

If the world owes much to the Yankee inventor it is none the less indebted to his inseparable coadjutor, the jackknife.

In the eighteenth century America had no clusters of cities and towns as it has today. Most of its people lived along the eastern seacoast where ships brought cloth, tools, gunpowder, coffee, sugar, salt and other products from overseas and carried away wool and flax and other raw materials to be made into useful articles abroad.

The interior of the country was mostly a wilderness. The first census of the United States, taken in 1790, revealed a total population of about four million, and only two or three thousand of these lived in what we now call the midwestern states. One reason for this was that there were no roads crisscrossing the country, and the people who ventured west had to break trails through forests, cross rivers and mountains, fight Indians and face other dangers which made travel risky and difficult.

It is estimated that about 90 per cent of the four million Americans worked on the land, raising crops and livestock. In other words, about nine out of every ten people were farmers. The rest included merchants, doctors, lawyers, shipbuilders, fishermen, blacksmiths, carpenters, shoemakers—that is, men who operated business enterprises in or near the coastal centers of population.

This meant that the farmers were compelled to be craftsmen. They were isolated from towns and cities, transportation was poor or entirely lacking, so family needs had to be supplied by the family itself. Food crops were mostly for home use because markets were too hard to reach. Plows and other farming implements were made by hand, along with shoes for the whole family. The women spun wool and flax to make the family's clothes; they also helped to plow and plant the fields, milked cows, churned butter and made candles and soap.

Homemade soap required the use of lye, which the farmer obtained by "leaching" wood ashes. Hardwood trees were cut down and burned, the ashes were put into barrels or tubs, and water was drained through the ashes. This leaching process produced lye, and by boiling water out of the lye in a big pot the farmer obtained "pot ash," which we now write as a single word, potash.

Sometimes men from the populated areas traveled through the countryside and bought quantities of potash from farmers, which they hauled to the shipping centers and sold in England and other countries for the manufacture of soap and glass. For the farmer a tremendous amount of labor was involved. A whole acre of hardwood trees had to be felled and burned in order to obtain a single ton of potash, for which he received twenty or twenty-five dollars.

An improvement in the making of "pot ash" was the basis for the very first patent issued under the first Federal Patent Act, passed by Congress on April 10, 1790. The patent was issued to Samuel Hopkins of Vermont.

Farmers also made medicines and ointments from roots, herbs, barks and berries, since they had no access to drugstores. There were no department stores or supermarkets, no organized real estate firms or building contractors. The people who settled on the land cut down trees, sawed them into boards and built their own houses, made their own tables, chairs, cabinets, desks, beds and other furnishings, even including wooden spoons, plates and bowls.

Thus, by necessity, the early settlers in America were artisans in many fields. They had to be jacks-of-all-trades in order to be self-sufficient and to live in bearable surroundings. They were the prize do-it-yourselfers of the New World, and today much of their beautiful handiwork is sold at fabulous prices in antique shops and fine furniture stores.

Benjamin Franklin once wrote a guide entitled *Information To Those Who Would Remove to America*. It included this advice:

. . . Much less it is advisable for a person to go thither [to America] who has no other quality to recommend him but his birth. In Europe it has indeed its value; but it is a commodity that cannot be carried to a worse market than that of America, where people do not inquire concerning a stranger, *What is he?* but, *What can he do?* If he has any useful art he is welcome; and if he exercises it and behaves well, he will be respected by all that know him; but a mere man of quality, who, on that account, wants to live upon the public, by some office or salary, will be despised and disregarded. The husbandman is in honor there, and even the mechanic, because their employments are useful. The people have a saying that God Almighty is himself a mechanic, the greatest in the universe; and He is respected and admired more for the variety, ingenuity and utility of His handiworks than for the antiquity of his family. . . . In short, America is the land of labor, and by no means what the English call *Lubberland*, and the French *Pays de Cocagne*, where the streets are said to be paved with half-peck loaves, the houses tiled with pancakes, and where the fowls fly about ready roasted, crying, Come eat me! . . . .

As more settlers arrived from abroad and communities grew, more merchants set up shops and stores and began to employ some of the local craftsmen. For example, a storekeeper would pay a carpenter to make chairs, or he would furnish iron to a blacksmith to be shaped into tools, hinges or other completed metal products for sale.

Some families bought land near brooks and streams and built mills for grinding grain into meal and flour, called "grist." The wooden water wheels used for power were, of course, fashioned by local carpenters.

Others operated water-powered sawmills where lumber could be cut much more quickly than by muscle power. The farmer who could not haul logs to a sawmill had to cut boards by hand.

While the Americans were struggling to produce the necessities of life with their hands and homemade tools, the British were gradually getting away from such slow, clumsy methods, thanks to the ingenuity of certain inventors whose new ideas for labor-saving devices were destined to change the whole way of life for Western civilization.

CHAPTER 2

The British Are Going

Have you ever heard the expression, "the distaff side"? The distaff side means the female branch of the family, and the expression comes from the fact that for centuries women spun wool, flax and cotton by using a distaff and spindle. The distaff was a short forked stick or a wooden framework on which the long fibers were wound and from which the fibers were connected to the spindle (a carrot-shaped block). The woman usually held the distaff under her left arm and the spindle in her right hand. With her right hand she rotated the spindle, using her left to twist the fibers from the distaff into yarn which was gradually wound around the spindle.

The distaff was made obsolete by the spinning wheel, whose own date and place of origin are not definitely known. There is evidence that spinning wheels were in use in the Orient long before the eighteenth century, when they became popular in Europe and America.

In England, as in America, farm families used their own skills to produce the necessities. They raised and sheared sheep, washed the wool and carded it (straightened the fibers), spun it into yarn, wove the yarn into cloth on the family loom, and made clothes for father, mother and children, all by hand. Spinning was virtually an occupation for a family's unmarried daughters, who were therefore called "spinsters," a term still used (interchangeably with "old maid") to describe an unmarried woman.

When the yarn was spun it was ready to be woven into cloth. In the mid-eighteenth century the cloth sold by English merchants was made on looms hand-operated by weavers in their own cottages, and clothmaking was known as a "cottage industry." Weaving was faster than spinning, and often the family could not spin yarn quickly enough to keep up with the loom. In 1733 this production lag between spinner and weaver grew even wider, thanks to a new idea conceived by young John Kay, of Bury, in Lancashire, England.

Kay's invention was called "the flying shuttle." Before it came into use a weaver operated the shuttle of his loom by pushing it manually from side to side, carrying the horizontal threads (called "weft," later "woof") across the vertical ("warp") threads. John Kay designed and built a time-and-labor-saving shuttle which, by connected cords, could be thrown swiftly to right and left merely by a sharp flick of a wooden peg or "fly pin."

Later, Kay's son Robert invented a "drop-box," which enabled a weaver to use any of three shuttles, each containing a different colored weft, without the trouble of taking them from and replacing them in the lathe.

The flying shuttle speeded up weaving so much that the spinners fell much farther behind in supplying the needed yarn, and looms were often idle while weavers waited and merchants pleaded for more finished material.

John Kay's invention was quite simple, but it marked the

beginning of a movement that would change the lives of people throughout the world. The flying shuttle was the prologue to what British economist Arnold Toynbee called "The Industrial Revolution"—an era in which machinery did the work formerly done by hand, and did it faster, cheaper, and frequently better than ever before. In other words, the so-called Industrial Revolution was really a Mechanical Evolution.

Although the Industrial Revolution was not a military conflict, it was marked by a full share of violence. For instance, when word spread that Kay's flying shuttle enabled one weaver to do the work formerly done by two or three, the Lancashire weavers became fearful and defiant. They met to discuss their problem.

"If the blasted thing ain't broke up it'll be our ruin, it will!" one said.

"Aye!" another agreed. "A few of us might have work, but the others will starve."

"Then we all know wot's got to be done, don't we, lads?"

There were nods and mutterings of agreement. "All right then—let's do it!"

Together they marched to Kay's home, an inflexible mob carrying clubs and hammers, as grim and relentless as any attacking army. At the house they knocked on the door and were admitted by Kay himself. Pushing him aside they swarmed through the tiny rooms, and wherever they came upon the models or parts of his invention they smashed them to splinters with their weapons. They tore up his sketches, wrecked some of his furniture and left the place a shambles. Kay tried to stop them, but against such a mob his muscle and his pleadings were as futile as the cry of a lamb brought to slaughter.

Beaten and discouraged, John Kay soon went to France to live and continue his work, but he died in that country without creating any new device more significant than his flying shuttle.

The unfortunate attack on Kay and the destruction of his work were destined to be repeated against others in the years to come, and for the same principal fear—that new machines would throw men out of work. In each case, however, the mechanical enemies proved to be the salvation of the working classes, because each new invention brought about a resulting expansion of industry and a demand for more and more manpower. Even now, in the latter half of the twentieth century, American workers continue to echo the old, old cry that new and improved machines will drive them to idleness and unemployment.

Some of Kay's new shuttles had been purchased by weavers before the raid on his home and were in successful use. Others were made and gradually accepted by more and more craftsmen, and the clothmakers plodded on peacefully as before, until their world was once again upset, this time by one of their own, a poor weaver named James Hargreaves, of Blackburn.

One day in 1764 Hargreaves was walking home from town with a supply of cotton which he had bought for his loom. As he opened the front door of his cottage his wife, Jenny, seated at her spinning wheel, was apparently startled, and she moved so quickly that she upset the wheel. Hargreaves saw that the spindle was in an upright position but kept turning and that the thread in Jenny's hand was still spinning.

"What's the matter?" his wife asked. "Why are you staring so? I'm all right. I was just startled some."

"It's the spindle," he said. "In that position it was still turning."

"There's no harm," Jenny said.

"No, no harm. But do you know something? If I could set up a whole row of spindles, all connected to one wheel—why, one spinster could do the work of four or five!"

Excited about his idea, Hargreaves set about making it a reality. He built a frame on which he mounted eight upright spindles. Another wooden device, something like a clamp, had eight rolls to be spun and was held by the spinner in the left hand while she used the right to turn the wheel that made the spindles rotate swiftly.

The invention worked perfectly, and with it the production of yarn in the Hargreaves' cottage took an eightfold jump. Realizing that he had solved the problem of the production lag between weaver and spinner, Hargreaves decided to keep his invention secret and build up his output and his profits. When he began to bring unusually big quantities of cloth to market, his fellow weavers became curious and suspicious.

"How can you do so much?" they asked. "How can Jenny spin so much yarn in so short a time?"

Hargreaves tried to joke about it, and when pressed for serious answers made them as evasive as possible. Either he confided in close friends about his invention, or Jenny did, or some visitor to the cottage saw it. In any event, his secret was discovered, and whispers that wafted from weaver to weaver soon grew into angry mutterings.

"It's the work of the devil, it is," the weavers said. "One spinster doing the work of eight, you say? 'Twill be the ruin of us all."

"So it will—unless we smash it!" someone said.

The workers' solution was the same as that for John Kay's flying shuttle. In true mob spirit the weavers broke into the Hargreaves cottage and hacked his invention to bits, strewing the floor with splinters and tangled yarn.

"Mind you don't build another one!" they warned. "If you do, we'll give it the same."

But the power of men is not great enough to destroy creative talents and ideas that mark progress in a civilized society. James and Jenny Hargreaves moved to Nottingham, where he built another multispindle device, and eventually (in 1770) he applied for and received a patent on it. As a tribute to his industrious wife he called his contraption a "spinning jenny."

When news of the invention spread, a few weavers in Nottingham and neighboring towns realized that for every person thrown out of work at the hand-operated spinning wheel, the demand for raw material created by the jenny would provide employment for two or more. Gradually the jenny came into wider use in the English textile world.

There was one difficulty, however. The yarn spun by the jenny was too soft, too lacking in strength and too coarse to be used for the warp (the longitudinal threads) in a loom, and it was still necessary for the weavers to use handmade linen and woolen threads for the warp. This problem was solved by a barber's apprentice named Richard Arkwright.

Born on December 23, 1732, at Preston, Lancashire, Richard Arkwright was the youngest of thirteen children. As a boy he became a barber's assistant, and when he finished his apprenticeship at the age of eighteen he opened his own barber shop. Business was so poor that he sold the shop and traveled from town to town buying human hair for use in making wigs, but this was also unprofitable and he soon gave it up.

Young Arkwright married and decided to settle down—but to what? At that time there was considerable interest among British inventors in a search for a perpetual motion machine (a search which continues today), and Arkwright turned his talents in that direction. His wife, however, argued that he should return to barbering or wigmaking, or go into some other "genteel trade" and not waste his time with foolish experiments. After all, inventions were created by educated men, and Richard Arkwright knew little of even simple reading and writing.

In conversations with other inventors and local weavers, Arkwright learned of the urgent need for a way to produce thread fine enough and strong enough to be used as warp in a loom. He gave up his perpetual motion experiments and plunged into an all-out effort to find the much-sought spinning secret. He built model after model, suffered failure after failure. Except for food and the barest necessities, his money was drained away for materials and supplies for his experiments. Over and over, his wife begged him to give up his "useless pursuits," but the search had become almost an obsession and Arkwright was determined to succeed.

His experiments overshadowed everything else. In appearance he became shabby and unkempt. His friends deserted him. His money was practically gone, yet he refused to give up or listen to his wife's pleas. One day, returning home from a walk, he found his models broken to splinters, yarn strewn over the floor, and his wife standing triumphantly in the midst of the debris.

Whether Arkwright grew violent or whether there was an agonized quarrel, the records show only that Mrs. Arkwright's havoc resulted in the couple's separation. Arkwright left his wife, taking what material and equipment he could salvage, and resumed his work. In 1767 he became friendly with a watchmaker of Warrington named John Kay (*not* the inventor of the flying shuttle).

At long last Arkwright designed a machine which he was sure would answer his purpose, and with John Kay's help in making the necessary parts he built a working model. Its principle was reasonably simple. There were two pairs of rollers, one pair revolving at a faster speed than the other. The yarn passed over the first, or slow, rollers and was drawn into and around the faster-moving pair, with the result that it was pulled taut and fashioned into strong, fine thread. Its diameter could be controlled by the roller tension and speeds.

Arkwright wanted to place his model on public exhibition, but he himself was so ragged and dirty that two or three remaining friends pooled enough money to buy him a presentable suit of clothes. The model was put on display in the parlor of a house owned by the grammar school in his own town of Preston, and several spinners and weavers came to see it. Once again, like Kay and Hargreaves, Richard Arkwright listened to the resentful comments of those who feared unemployment. Angry noises became outspoken threats: "Take your infernal machine and yourself away from here, or we'll run you out!" In other words, to his fellow citizens Arkwright and his invention were public enemies.

Disappointed but not discouraged, he moved to Nottingham in 1768, along with John Kay and another friend, John Smalley. The three built a small mill (probably with funds provided by Kay and Smalley), installed Arkwright's new devices and used horses for motive power. The spinners in Nottingham, who were making warp threads by hand, soon ganged up for the now-familiar reason—fear of losing jobs— and descended on the mill. Fighting off Arkwright and his two friends, they destroyed the machinery and ordered the trio to get out of town.

Poor Arkwright! After what he himself called "many years of intense and painful application," he had succeeded, only to be defeated by the very workers his invention was designed to help.

In 1769 Arkwright obtained a patent on his device, but he had no money to build another mill. Unwilling to quit, he set out to find someone who would have enough faith in him and his invention to finance it, and in 1771 he found his man, or rather, his men.

Jedediah Strutt, whose quaint name was respected by farmers and scholars alike, was six years older than Richard Arkwright. As a youth he was a farmer, like his father, but in his twenties his brother-in-law had aroused his interest in a need to produce ribbed cloth on a stocking frame, and Strutt invented the successful "Derby ribbing machine." Strutt and his brother-in-law started a factory in Derby, and in 1762 Strutt took in a partner named Samuel Need.

In Arkwright's quest for help he met Sam Need, to whom he explained his invention. Need brought him to Strutt, who was so impressed that Arkwright was taken into the partnership, and in 1771 the three built a fairly large factory at Cromford, Derbyshire, and installed Arkwright's devices. Because the machinery was powered by a water wheel it came to be called a "water frame," and the thread which it spun was known as "water twist." Some also called the machine a "jack frame."

Arkwright later made and patented several improvements in the frame, and although no frightened workmen came to destroy the machinery, other difficulties popped up unexpectedly. Competitors of the partners, operating in old-fashioned ways, influenced various manufacturers against doing business with Arkwright and his associates, even though their thread was admittedly superior. Others, aware of the efficiency of Arkwright's machine, duplicated it for their own use and refused to pay him for his patents or to pay royalties.

A number of court battles followed, with Arkwright fighting valiantly to protect the invention that had brought him so much heartache and trouble. In the end he emerged the winner, and not only sold big quantities of thread but also began to build more mills—and with the coming of success he started to improve his reading and writing when he was fifty years old.

Before Richard Arkwright's several mills dotted the English countryside, it was the custom for manufacturers to have certain portions of their products made in different places. Carding was done at one location, spinning at another, weaving somewhere else. Arkwright, however, introduced a "modern" system by having all necessary production operations performed under one factory roof. Unfortunately for his employees he paid little attention to such essentials as proper light, ventilation and sanitation, and as a result the health of many of his workers was seriously impaired.

Arkwright's personal story has a happy ending, for besides becoming a very wealthy manufacturer he was knighted by King George III. Sir Richard Arkwright died in Cromford on August 3, 1792.

Textile machinery was not the only field in which man's social, economic and political future was being shaped. In the midst of the Kay-Hargreaves-Arkwright era, power for operating machinery was generally furnished by horses or water, but in 1769 a young Scot named James Watt obtained a patent for a steam engine—a device that was to change our whole civilization by giving the industrial world muscles of iron and steel and the power to make them work.

James Watt was not the inventor of the steam engine. Steam as a source of power was known long before the time of Christ. In the sixteenth century, according to a Spanish claim, steam was used by a Spanish naval officer named Blasco de Garay to turn paddle wheels on a ship. In 1630 a patent was issued to David Ramsay in England for an invention which would make any sort of mills "goe on standing waters by continual motion, without help of wind, water, or horse; to make boats, shippes and barges to goe against strong wind and tide; to raise water from low places and mynes and coal pitts by a new waie never yet in use."

Up to 1663 steam was used in England for light work, such as the turning of spits, but in 1663 Edward Somerset, Marquis of Worcester, supposedly wrote a book called *Century* in which he described one hundred inventions of his own, covering a multitude of subjects, including steam-operated mechanical devices. Some historians claim that there was no such person as Somerset, while others insist that he was the true inventor of the steam engine.

In 1702 one Thomas Savery invented a steam-operated vacuum pump, using a principle described by Somerset. Savery's pump was designed to drain water from mines, but it required such extremely high pressure that some of his boilers exploded, and mineowners refused to buy it.

At any rate, steam as a motive power was known long before James Watt showed how it could be turned to practical and effective use. Watt's interest in steam might never have been aroused had it not been for a breakdown in a steam engine invented by Thomas Newcomen and used for operating mine pumps. Newcomen and Savery had joined forces, and together devised a pump that worked satisfactorily.

A model of one of these pump-engines was used for instruction purposes in the University of Glasgow, Scotland, in 1763. One day it broke down and was brought for repair to James Watt, a twenty-seven-year-old instrument-maker whose shop was on the university grounds.

Watt not only repaired the machine, but also conceived an idea for making it far more efficient. In the Newcomen engine steam was forced into a cylinder and operated a piston. After each operation a stream of cold water had to be injected to cool the cylinder so the piston would return to its original position. Then the next jet of steam had to heat the cylinder walls, resulting in some condensation. The resulting operation was necessarily slow.

Watt sought a way to speed it up, but not until 1765 did he find the solution. He designed a *separate* chamber in which the steam would be condensed, and by this method the cylinder with the piston would remain hot.

Bit by bit Watt made other improvements until he had finally fashioned a model of a practical, efficient steam engine, which he patented in 1769.

Watt hadn't a penny to manufacture a full-scale engine, so he went into partnership with John Roebuck, owner of an ironworks, who was to finance the venture and receive two-thirds of the profits. However, Roebuck soon became bankrupt and this partnership ended.

Young Watt temporarily abandoned work on the engine, partly because of lack of money, partly because it was impossible to get handmade cylinders that were properly bored. In order to support his family, Watt took whatever jobs he could get, but he returned to the steam engine as the result of a meeting with Matthew Boulton, wealthy owner of the Soho Foundry Engineering Works in Birmingham, England.

Boulton was experienced enough to see that Watt's ideas were sound and his engine practicable, so the partnership of Boulton & Watt was established. With Boulton's money Watt's engine was completed, proved to be workable, and the manufacture of more engines began, even though the cylinders were not as perfectly bored as they should be.

In trying to sell engines to mineowners to replace horses for pulling or lifting heavy loads, Boulton and Watt discovered that they could not make the owners understand the meaning of pounds of steam pressure, so in their sales talks they spoke of the engine's power in terms of the number of horses it could replace. To make an accurate estimate for this purpose, Watt conducted experiments which showed that one horse could lift a weight of 33,000 pounds one foot in one minute. In other words, this was "one horsepower," a term which has survived to our own day.

Gradually Watt's engines came into use in mining, manufacturing and transportation, and Watt lived in prosperity and contentment until he died on August 19, 1819.

Watt's engine was not strictly original but was in fact a great improvement upon the ideas of Savery, Newcomen and others. A somewhat similar situation came about in the textile industry while Richard Arkwright, inventor of the water frame, was fighting the legal battles mentioned earlier in this chapter. A young Lancashire lad who operated a spinning jenny in a mill decided that he could improve upon this creation of James Hargreaves.

Night after night young Samuel Crompton spent all of his spare time and money in experimenting, and in 1779, after nearly six years, he succeeded in developing a machine which would spin yarn fine enough for the making of muslin. Although the machine was original and the first of its kind, it actually combined certain principles of the spinning jenny and of Arkwright's machine, and because of this "cross" between "the jack and the jenny," the invention became known as "Crompton's mule" (because a real mule is a cross between a horse and a jackass).

Crompton's mule was a success, but he was too poor to pay for a patent, so he agreed to reveal his secret to certain manufacturers who were to pay him for the use of the machine. Instead of the sum agreed upon, they paid him only $300. Later the British Parliament awarded him about $20,000, which he used to go into the textile business. As a businessman he was a failure, and in his last years he lived on a small annuity purchased by his friends. Crompton died in poverty on June 26, 1827.

In 1784, at a time when Richard Arkwright's success was assured, a Kentish minister named Edmund Cartwright, who chanced to be visiting at Matlock in Derby, joined in a casual conversation with some gentlemen from Manchester. The talk soon turned to Arkwright's newfangled machinery.

Said one of the strangers, "One day Arkwright's patents will expire and then so many mills will be built and so much cotton will be spun that there will never be enough hands to weave it."

"In that case," the Reverend Mr. Cartwright said, "Mr. Arkwright will have to set his wits to work to build a power weaving mill."

The men laughed at such an impossibility, and the talk turned to other subjects. The minister did not forget the conversation, however, and a few months later he wondered whether or not he could make a mechanical device that would imitate the movements of a human weaver's hands on a loom.

Cartwright knew nothing about weaving and had never even seen a loom in action, but he built a contraption that was so big and heavy that it took the muscle power of two men to work it. After he obtained a patent on his invention on April 4, 1785, he discovered that ordinary looms were much lighter than his, and easier to operate, so he made a better model incorporating his new ideas and took out another patent in 1787.

The Cartwright power loom was a success, but like others before him Cartwright was beset by the familiar bugaboo of fear. He sold four hundred of his power looms to a manufacturer in Manchester. Soon after they were installed a mob of weavers, yelling and brandishing torches, swooped down upon the mill at night, set it on fire and retreated to watch it burn to the ground. No, sir—no new machines were going to put *them* in the jobless ranks!

Despite such thoughtless opposition the flying shuttle, the spinning jenny, the water frame, the Crompton mule, the steam engine and the power loom brought about significant changes in English industrial and social life. The demand for cotton created work for thousands of men to plant, grow and handle it. New factories required hundreds of workers for spinning and weaving, which, in turn, meant more jobs for carpenters, smiths and others to erect buildings and make the needed equipment. More ships and sailors were needed to carry raw materials from the colonies and other lands and to export the finished goods. The textile business was booming.

In the face of this progress, many weavers and spinners were still opposed to mechanization, not only in England but in France and Germany as well. In France, for example, a young weaver of silk named Marie Jacquard in 1800 invented a loom attachment which simplified the weaving of figured patterns in silk. The French government brought Jacquard to Paris from his home in Lyons so that he could operate his device as a government employee and could train others to use it.

In 1804 Jacquard returned to Lyons and immediately became the target for gangs of weavers who shouted that his invention would bring starvation to all of them. When they threatened to destroy his looms in Lyons, the government sent troops to safeguard the mills. Even then the mob managed to steal one of his looms and smash it, and soon they seized Jacquard himself and dragged him through the streets, intending to drown him in the Rhone River. The crowd's shouts attracted the attention of some of the soldiers, who rescued Jacquard.

Later, when the weavers of Lyons heard about the increase of jobs in other cities due to Jacquard's invention they offered no further opposition to the installation of the looms in Lyons, and Jacquard was permitted to live in peace in the town of his birth.

The weavers and spinners were not the only ones who fought the spread of mechanized industry. Rich and aristocratic landowners were opposed to the growing wealth of "common" manufacturers and tradesmen—and some of the manufacturers themselves tried to keep others from building new factories, fearing that so much thread and cloth would be produced that prices would tumble, and profits along with them.

Theirs was a losing battle, because the new industry meant progress, and progress was more powerful than its enemies. The inventions of John Kay, James Hargreaves, Sir Richard Arkwright, James Watt, Samuel Crompton and Edmund Cartwright revolutionized the entire British textile industry and brought into existence the so-called factory system.

The British government, aware that the inventions for spinning and weaving were created and used exclusively in England, with a few in France, decided to keep them from spreading to other countries and thus avoid competition. Accordingly, in 1781 the British Parliament amended an existing law to provide that

. . . any person who packed or put on board, or caused to be brought to any place in order to be put on any vessel for exportation, any machine, engine, tool, press, paper, utensil or implement or any part thereof, which now is or hereafter may be used in the woollen, cotton, linen or silk manufacture of the kingdom, or goods wherein wool, cotton, linen or silk are used, or any model or plan of such machinery, tool, engine, press, utensil or implement, shall forfeit every such machine . . . and all goods packed therewith, and £200, and suffer imprisonment for one year."

In other words, no person was permitted to take out of England any tool or machinery used in the textile industry, or any drawings or plans of such tools or machinery. In addition, the government proposed to keep from leaving the country any British textile worker who was familiar with the new mechanical devices.

All sorts of tricks were used by Americans in attempts to smuggle textile machinery out of England. Some bought the equipment on the pretext that they were going into business in Britain; then they dismantled it, packed pieces separately in crates labeled "Glassware" or "Farm Implements," and shipped the boxes to France, intending to reship them to America.

A writer at the time reported, "British agents and the Royal Navy managed to intercept almost all such shipments, and skilled workers who attempted to slip away with drawings or models were apprehended on the high seas and brought back. Passengers leaving English for American ports were thoroughly searched by Customs agents before boarding ship."

If it had not been for the luck and phenomenal memory of one English youth, the Industrial Revolution in the United States might have been delayed for several years and might not have begun, as it did, in 1791.

CHAPTER 3

Thankee, Yankee!

Cloth woven on the British power looms was produced in such quantities that it could be shipped to America and sold at prices so low that it was almost useless for American spinners and weavers to try to make a living by their spinning wheels and hand-worked looms. The Americans heard about the new industrialism in England, but were powerless to rent, borrow, buy or steal any of the textile machinery because of the strict British laws and the watchful eyes of the agents of the Crown.

At the time when Jedediah Strutt and Richard Arkwright built their water-powered mill at Cromford, a three-year-old boy named Samuel Slater lived with his parents on an estate adjoining that of Mr. Strutt. The Strutts and Slaters were good friends—so good that when young Samuel Slater was only fourteen years old, Jed Strutt arranged to hire the youth as a clerk in his new stocking factory, being built only a mile from the Slater property. With his father's consent young Sam began his clerkship.

After a year the boy decided that he preferred manufacturing to clerical work, and Mr. Strutt agreed that Sam could be indentured (bound by a contract) as an apprentice cotton spinner until he was twenty-one years old.

Young Slater not only put in full days at work in the mill, but also spent extra hours at night and on Sundays studying the machinery and seeking ways to make it more efficient. After some experiments he succeeded in creating improved designs for parts of the spinning operation, and throughout his seven-year apprenticeship his eagerness to learn was matched only by his enthusiasm and growing ambition. Even before he was twenty-one he was promoted to superintendent of the Strutt-Arkwright hosiery mill at Milford.

Having reached the job of superintendent, how much higher could he go? Time had run out on the Arkwright patents, which were now available to anyone, and there was a resulting building boom in new textile factories. Competition was terrific, and young Slater's knowledge and observation of the expanding industry convinced him that it would be difficult, if not impossible, to carve out a really successful career as an individual in England.

One day he happened to see a Philadelphia newspaper which carried a story saying that the state of Pennsylvania in October, 1788, had paid a hundred pounds to a man named John Hague, who had designed a machine for carding cotton. In the same paper he saw advertisements and notices to the effect that anyone who could introduce the British cloth-manufacturing processes in America would reap handsome profits.

Slater began to think about going to the United States, but the risks he faced made him hesitate. Finally, in September, 1789, some three months after his twenty-first birthday, he told his mother he was going to London for a brief visit. In London he changed clothes to make himself look as much like a farm boy as possible. This was not too difficult, for he was six feet tall, muscular, and had a good crop of blond hair and a ruddy, outdoor complexion.

He made sure that he carried no written or printed matter except his indenture papers, which he concealed, perhaps in his shoe. His most valuable possession was a plan for a modern cotton mill—and it was invisible, for it existed only in his remarkable memory.

In London he wrote his mother that he was on the way to America, then went to his ship, trying not to betray his nervousness. No one questioned him, and he completed the uneventful sixty-six day voyage to New York in November, 1789. His plan to go to Philadelphia failed to materialize when he saw the clothmaking "New York Manufacturing Company" on Vesey Street in New York City. He landed a job there, but the equipment was antiquated, the owners were not interested in modernizing it, and Slater resolved to seek his future elsewhere.

One day he struck up a conversation with the captain of a ship carrying passengers between New York and Providence, Rhode Island, who told him about a Quaker in Providence who had invested considerable money in spinning machines that didn't work. The Quaker's name was Moses Brown (who subsequently helped to found Brown University).

In a letter to Moses Brown dated December 2, 1789, sent from "No. 37 Golden Hill, New York," Slater wrote that he could give satisfaction in making machinery or yarn as good "as any that is made in England." He described his service with Arkwright and Strutt and said that he would like "to erect a perpetual card and spinning machine."

Replying on December 10, Moses Brown wrote that his machines were imperfect. "We hardly know what to say to thee," the letter went on, "but if thou thought thou couldst perfect and conduct them to profit, if thou wilt come and do it, thou shalt have all the profits made of them and above the interest of the money they cost, and the wear and tear of them. . . ."

This was the opening of a door to a great adventure, and Slater left New York with a pounding heart and a youthful impatience at the slowness of travel. He reached snow-covered Providence on January 18, 1790, and met elderly, soft-spoken Moses Brown, whose broad-brimmed Quaker hat came barely to Slater's shoulder. The old man peered up at the young man through his square spectacles, and even at this first meeting each must have felt a kinship for the other.

Brown was in partnership with his son-in-law, William Almy, and in a one-horse sleigh Brown and Slater drove to the Almy & Brown mill in the nearby village of Pawtucket. Slater's enthusiasm was jolted when he saw the machinery in the mill. Compared to the Arkwright equipment it was laughable—perhaps pitiful was the better word.

"These machines are useless," Slater said. "I would not even try to work with them."

Anxiously Moses Brown said, "But thee could make changes? Arrange them as they should be?"

"No." Slater shook his head slowly. "It would only be wasted time."

They left the mill and went to the Pawtucket home of Brown's friend, Oziel Wilkinson, a blacksmith whose ability, supplemented by a water-powered shop, had gained him a fine reputation as a craftsman and a thriving ironwork businessman.

After some deliberation, Moses Brown suggested that young Slater dismantle the imperfect machinery and work with Wilkinson to build a whole new set, using whatever parts could be salvaged from the old. If he succeeded, and the machinery worked satisfactorily, Slater would become a half-owner of the mill with William Almy and Smith Brown, a cousin of Moses'.

Slater agreed, became a boarder in the Wilkinson home, and later married Wilkinson's daughter, Hannah.

In the spring of 1790 the twenty-two-year-old Englishman began work on his project. He had no drawings of tools or machines, no models for use as patterns, no measurements—only his memory and experience. From sketches which Slater drew on rough boards with chalk, Wilkinson fashioned the metal parts he needed; a local wheelwright turned oak logs into wheels, posts or other necessary wooden pieces; and a mechanic friend of Wilkinson's made cards for the carding machine. Cards were pieces of leather studded with short, strong wire teeth which were pulled through cotton or wool fibers to unsnarl and make them straight, ready for spinning.

In the late autumn of 1790 the new machinery was about ready. From memory alone Slater had designed and built a modern spinning mill with seventy-two spindles. A week before Christmas the machinery was connected to a water wheel outside the mill on the Blackstone River, but Slater had to smash the ice around the wheel before it would turn.

And turn it did. The whirring machinery was a welcome sound in the small mill, and on December 20, 1790, Slater and his partners were happy witnesses to the operations of the first automatic cotton-spinning mill in the United States.

Slater's success came at an opportune time. The Constitution of the United States had been ratified only two years earlier and provided for duties to be imposed upon various goods from foreign countries. The British, who had exported great quantities of cloth for sale in America at extremely low prices, would now have to pay a tariff to get their merchandise into the United States. This meant that they must raise their prices in order to make a profit. As a result, American clothmakers could compete with their British rivals.

Within a month after his mill opened, Samuel Slater had hired nine employees, most of whom were children ranging in age from four to twelve years. Their pay: 80¢ to $1.40 a week. Child labor was a common practice in England, and it was natural for Slater to adopt it for the new mill. Unlike most British manufacturers, however, he made sure that the children were well-fed and properly cared for, and to supplement their physical welfare he established the first Sunday school in New England, where his young workers could learn not only the teachings of the Bible, but the three R's as well.

Samuel Slater, who introduced the factory system to America, has been called "The Father of American Manufacturers." He built other mills in New England, and when he died in 1835 his estate was valued at well over a million dollars.

Although the Pawtucket spinning mill was a success, the weaving of cloth was still done by hand, and the yarn output of the mill was far greater than weavers could use. In addition, the British and Irish were still sending shiploads of cloth to America to be sold at low prices to defeat competition, even with the tariff. Slater and his partners continued to sell their yarn throughout New England and managed to prosper, but it was evident that automatic spinning mills would not reach their full potential until there were power looms to handle the thousands of pounds of yarn produced by the spindles.

Before the first power loom shuttled its way into America's textile business, industrial progress took another giant step forward through a Yankee schoolteacher with a flair for the mechanical arts.

Eli Whitney, the son of a farmer who was also a good mechanic, was born December 8, 1765, in Westboro, Massachusetts. As a boy Eli showed that he had inherited some of his father's mechanical aptitude, for he spent hours experimenting with tools. When he was only twelve he made a violin, and one day he secretly borrowed his father's pocket watch, brought it to his room, took it completely apart and reassembled it perfectly. In his early teens, while grownups were fighting a war for their independence from England, young Eli helped his neighbors by hammering out iron nails and other articles needed for building and farming.

After completing a local grammar school education he earned money by teaching in various country schools, but he had a desire to improve his own education so he made application and was accepted at Yale University in New Haven, Connecticut. He earned at least part of his tuition by spare-time tutoring and by repairing scientific equipment, furniture and other material at the school. He graduated in 1792 at the age of twenty-seven, expecting to become a teacher or lawyer.

A friend, Phineas Miller, also a Yale graduate, told Eli about a private school in South Carolina that needed a tutor. Miller was employed as manager of the estate of the late Revolutionary General Nathanael Greene, and Miller and the general's widow, Catherine, were preparing to go to the estate near Savannah, Georgia. Eli was invited to accompany them on his way to South Carolina, where he hoped to fill the tutoring job. With Miller and Mrs. Greene he boarded a sailing ship in New York, bound for Savannah—a voyage destined to change not only his own life but also the industrial life of his country.

During the voyage Whitney became very friendly with Mrs. Greene, and she was impressed by his fund of knowledge in many fields, including mechanics. Arriving in Savannah, the widow invited Whitney to be a guest at her home before continuing his journey, and he accepted.

While there, Whitney made a new kind of embroidery frame as a gift for Mrs. Greene, and told her about new and unusual ideas he had for other useful articles.

In a social gathering at the Greene house, a group of gentlemen talked about the depressed farming situation in Georgia. Whitney and Mrs. Greene were interested listeners.

"The land isn't suited to growing rice," one man said, "and if we don't find some other crop soon, we'll all be in real trouble."

"I certainly agree," another said. "But what other crop?"

A third answered, "It's a shame there isn't some good fast way to clean cotton. Cotton will grow like fury all through this area, and—"

"Yes," the first man interrupted, "and you'd pile it to high heaven waiting for the seeds to be cleaned out to sell it."

They all nodded. "Someday somebody will find a machine to do it," one suggested.

The others laughed and one added, "I wish he'd come along soon. He could keep me from bankruptcy!"

Now Mrs. Greene spoke up. "He's right here, gentlemen." She pointed to Eli. "My friend Mr. Whitney can make anything. Come here and I'll show you."

She showed them the embroidery frame and described some of Whitney's other achievements and ideas. When the men politely suggested to Whitney that a seed-cleaning machine would benefit both country and inventor, he smiled. "Gentlemen," he said, "I've never even *seen* any raw cotton or cottonseed!"

Cottonseed was the big obstacle to the southern planters. It was not worth their while to grow big crops of cotton because it had to be picked by hand, and in order to sell it the seeds had to be removed from the fiber, also by hand, or squeezed by a crude arrangement of rollers which were far from satisfactory. One slave, working all day long, could clean about one pound of cotton. A machine that would make big quantities of seed-free cotton would be the salvation of the South, and Eli Whitney began to think about creating just such a machine.

Within ten days he had made a small model for experimentation. When it seemed satisfactory, Whitney built a full-scale machine that could be operated by one man to clean ten times as much cotton as one worker could clean manually in a day.

Whitney left promptly for Philadelphia, then the national capital, where he applied for a patent and hired several workmen to make additional machines. In Philadelphia on September 11, 1793, he wrote a letter to his father telling him about the invention and asking that it be kept a close secret by the Whitney family.

At that time Whitney did not know that his secret had already been revealed by Catherine Greene, who was so proud of her friend's achievement that she showed his model to several people. Some historians say that thieves broke into the Greene household at night and stole Whitney's device. Whatever happened, the secret did get out, and in a short time other people were making and selling machines patterned after Eli Whitney's cotton gin ("gin" was a contraction of "engine").

The principle of the cotton gin was quite simple. A cylinder, or drum, was studded with curved teeth of stiff iron wire with sharpened points and was turned by a handle or crank. (Later, circular saws replaced the toothed drum.) Facing this cylinder was a fixed receptacle in which raw cotton was placed. Between the cotton and the cylinder was a metal barrier with vertical teeth close together, something like a large fine comb.

Near the cylinder was a cylindrical brush which revolved four times faster than the spiked drum when the crank was turned.

In action, the sharp teeth of the rotating drum clawed at the cotton fibers between the vertical ribs of the comb. The fibers were pulled away, but the cotton seeds were too big to get through and merely piled up to be thrown away.

The revolving brush simply swept the cleaned cotton from the spikes on the rotating drum, keeping them clear of fibers.

Although Whitney obtained a patent in March, 1794, and went into partnership with Phineas Miller, he met ruin and disaster.

One big calamity broke in 1795. Early one morning a large New Haven factory in which Whitney and Miller had installed several cotton gins caught fire and burned to the ground. Writing to his father, Whitney reported that he had been away at the time and that upon his return "I found my property all in ashes! My shop, all my tools, material and work equal to twenty finished cotton machines all gone. The manner in which it took fire is altogether unaccountable."

Throughout the South new factories were springing up, equipped with Whitney's cotton gins without payment to Whitney. Whitney and Miller sued these rival manufacturers for patent infringement, but were generally unsuccessful. The

South had exploded into sudden prosperity, and no one was much concerned with the complaints of a lone Yankee inventor.

Until now the slaves on huge southern plantations were becoming liabilities. The principal crops were tobacco and rice, and there was a growing surplus of slaves for the amount of work to be done. A few planters had even freed some slaves to save money that must otherwise be spent for their food, clothes and shelter. When Whitney's cotton gin opened the way to a tremendous boom in southern agriculture, slaves were in great demand and played a vital role in the fast-growing cotton economy of the South.

When Whitney invented his machine in 1793, the entire United States cotton crop totaled only about 1,500,000 pounds and about 150,000 pounds of this was exported. Within seven years after his invention came into use the American cotton crop reached 35,000,000 pounds, about one-half of which (18,000,000 pounds) was exported yearly.

Realizing the wealth to be made from cotton, many of the younger men left the plantations of their parents and headed into the unpopulated wilderness, where they acquired thousands of acres of land on which they planted and harvested their own fluffy riches. Cotton was king, and the kingdom was rapidly expanding.

The riches that Eli Whitney had dreamed about as profits from his invention were never much more than dreams. Although he finally obtained awards totaling about $90,000, mostly as the result of court decisions in North and South Carolina and Tennessee, he had to spend most of this sum to carry on a multitude of other legal battles, few of which netted him anything except discouragement.

A crowning blow came from textile manufacturers in Manchester, England, who spread the propaganda that Whitney's gin so damaged the cotton fiber that it was useless for spinning. This unfounded and vicious charge drifted through the American textile industry like loose cotton in a high wind, and practically ruined Whitney's business. It took him some two years to make the industry realize that the charge was utterly false.

By 1798, only five years after he had completed his first model of the cotton gin, Whitney was tired of fighting. His idea had been stolen, his patents infringed, his factory burned down, his process libeled and most of his money spent for scores of legal battles. His despair was eloquently described in a letter he wrote in 1797, part of which says:

The extreme embarrassments which have for a long time been accumulating upon me are now become so great that it will be impossible for me to struggle against them many days longer. . . . Life is but short at best, and six or seven years out of the midst of it is, to him who makes it, an immense sacrifice. My most unremitted attention has been directed to our business. I have sacrificed to it other objects from which, before this time, I might certainly have gained twenty or thirty thousand dollars. My whole prospects have been embarked in it, with the expectation that I should before this time, have realized something from it.

Thomas Babington Macaulay, British statesman, writer and historian, once wrote, "What Peter the Great did to make Russia dominant, Eli Whitney's invention of the Cotton-Gin has more than equaled in its relation to the progress and power of the United States."

Surely few men of genius whose creative ability was of such tremendous benefit to their country have been as ill-treated as Eli Whitney and so poorly repaid. He did not even get a hearty "Thankee, Yankee!" from those who made fortunes from his invention. Happily, however, he turned to another activity that not only brought him rich rewards, but also blazed a trail to what history calls "The American System of Manufacture."

In the years immediately following the end of the War of Independence, the new government needed supplies to equip a standing military force. Guns were especially important and should be obtained in quantity, but there was no such thing as a gun factory. Rifles were handmade by individual craftsmen, the process was very slow and no two weapons were exactly alike.

In 1798 Eli Whitney, weary of fighting those who refused to keep their hands off his gin, conceived a new idea that would take him from gin to gun. Thanks to the help of his friend Oliver Wolcott, Secretary of the Navy, and armed only with an exciting idea, Whitney convinced government officials that he could produce ten thousand muskets in two years, at a cost of $13.40 each. Although he had no machines and no models, he had earned a reputation as a brilliant inventor, and on this basis the government entered into a contract with him for the ten thousand guns.

Whitney began immediately to build a gun factory in Whitneyville, near New Haven, Connecticut. First he designed a rifle. For each part of it, from stock to trigger, he made a cut-out pattern which a workman could use to fashion a corresponding piece in metal, just as a seamstress uses a paper pattern to cut and make a dress.

If the metal-cutting were chiseled by hand it was possible that one piece would not be exactly like another, as Whitney wanted it to be, so he designed a special "milling machine" with sharp curved steel teeth on a rotating wheel. In operation, a piece of metal covered by a pattern, or template, could be moved so that the teeth followed the outline of the pattern and made uniform cuts into the metal. This made it possible for even an inexperienced workman to do a job that heretofore required the skill of a master machinist, and there were only a few of the latter in the country.

When the first year of Whitney's contract ended he had produced only five hundred muskets, because he had spent most of the time designing and building his plant and special machinery. When the second and final contract year was up, he had failed to make the promised ten thousand guns, but he went to Washington to ask for an extension of time and an advance of money.

Government officials were at first reluctant to consider Whitney's requests, but changed their minds after he staged an unusual demonstration. While the Secretary of War and other officials watched, Whitney laid out ten separate piles of musket parts. Selecting pieces at random from the different piles, he quickly assembled ten complete rifles in perfect condition. So impressed was his official audience that Whitney was given his extension and an advance.

It took him about eight years to complete the ten thousand rifles, mostly because much of this time was devoted to improvements in his tools and machinery, but once the guns were delivered, the government ordered fifteen thousand more, which he completed within two years.

This was the beginning of mass production in the United States. It was not originated by Whitney, since it had been tried in France and England (though not on guns). Eli Whitney, however, made the idea practical, introduced the first power-driven machine tools and thus contributed a great upsurge to the Industrial Revolution in American manufacturing.

This time Whitney reaped a fortune from his business. When he died in 1825 the work was carried on by his nephews, son and grandson, and eventually the Whitney armory was taken over by the Winchester Repeating Arms Company, which is still in business in New Haven.

Whitney's cotton gin and mass production methods, Watt's steam engine and Samuel Slater's automatic spinning mill foreshadowed the start of a great new industrial age in America. Others following in their pioneering footsteps would build bigger and better factories. There would be demands for more cotton, wool and linen, providing material for good clothing at lower prices. To operate the mills the steam engine would replace horse and water power. Factories would make "cottage industry" obsolete, and people who once made a bare living for themselves and their families by handwork at home would be employed in the shops and paid regular wages that might enable them to buy not only necessities but also some of the luxuries once enjoyed only by the rich.

The rich would also benefit, for they could invest money in new factories and new inventions, although growing competition and mass production would compel them to make goods of better quality at lower prices in order to make their enterprises profitable—and profit was the principal concern of the capitalist.

All in all, the beginning of the Industrial Revolution in America held great promise for the future of the nation and its people, and there were even more marvels to come.

CHAPTER 4

Power Drives and Paddle Wheels

A hundred years before the word *automobile* came into use, a strange craft with the odd name of *Oruktor Amphibolos* ("Amphibious Digger") steamed across one and a half miles of Pennsylvania countryside to the shores of the Schuylkill River. Instead of wheels the thirty-foot craft, weighing some fifteen tons, traveled on rollers, and after it was eased into the river the rollers were removed and replaced by a kind of paddle wheel at the stern. Driven by a five-horsepower steam engine the scow headed for Philadelphia, to be used by the city authorities as a dredge and for cleaning docks. Its designer and builder was Oliver Evans. The year was 1804.

The *Oruktor Amphibolos* was an ancestor of the automobile and also one of the first successful American steamboats. It was probably the first mechanically propelled vehicle and the first amphibious craft in America.

The son of a farmer, Oliver Evans was born in Newport, Delaware, in 1755. At fourteen he was apprenticed to a wheelwright, and in his spare time he drew plans for new kinds of horse-drawn carriages. He had enough formal education to read and write, but little more. Whenever possible he borrowed books from friends about mechanics, history and politics, but his stingy employer refused to let the boy burn candles at night, so he read the books before the fireplace, in which he burned wood shavings to make bright light.

Oliver's older brothers operated a flour mill, and when they recognized his mechanical ability they made him their partner. Seeking to improve the business, Oliver invented new ways to use several labor-saving appliances for grinding, sifting and loading grain, not only increasing production but also reducing costs so that flour could be sold at lower prices. These inventions eliminated the need for most of the hired hands and constituted the world's first "automated" mill.

In the course of his reading Evans learned about Newcomen's work with steam engines, and he quickly realized that Newcomen's engine was little more than a pump in which a blast of steam created a vacuum, while air pressure alone drove the piston. Why not make the steam do real work? Why not, indeed! In experiments of his own in 1787 Evans designed what became known as a "double-acting, high-pressure" steam engine, in which steam at pressures of more than fifty pounds to the inch was applied to *both* sides of a piston.

This kind of steam engine, instead of being just a pump, had the power to drive other kinds of machines, which meant that factories would no longer have to use horses or be built near rivers to use water-powered machinery.

Evans invested all the money he had in building an engine and mill to grind plaster and saw marble. Although many people witnessed the successful demonstration of his engine, none wanted to buy or invest in it.

In 1804 he received the order from Philadelphia that resulted in his construction of the *Oruktor Amphibolos,* and when crowds turned out in Philadelphia to watch this craft waddle out of the river under its own power, Evans believed that he would get orders for more engines. He was wrong. Manufacturers weren't interested. Shipbuilders weren't interested. Nobody was interested, at least not enough to buy.

For the next several years Oliver Evans' livelihood came from a general store and foundry which he owned, and it was only shortly before he died in 1819 that his high-pressure steam engines gained public favor.

Some years before his death Evans made this prediction:

The time will come when people will travel in stages moved by steam engines from one city to another, almost as fast as birds can fly, 15 or 20 miles an hour. A carriage will start from Washington in the morning, the passengers will breakfast at Baltimore, dine at Philadelphia, and sup in New York the same day. . . . Two sets of railways will be laid, so nearly level as not in any way to deviate more than two degrees in a horizontal line, made of wood or stone, or smooth paths of broken stone or gravel, with a rail to guide the carriages so that they may pass each other in different directions and travel by night as well as by day. Engines will drive boats ten or twelve miles per hour and there will be many hundreds of steamboats running on the Mississippi.

Undoubtedly the idea of using steam engines to propel boats through the water seemed more sensible to some than trying to move carriages over the land. Roads were rutty and bumpy enough to break wheels, hills were steep, and most folks preferred to travel by boat when they could, even though the boat was pulled by mules at an agonizingly slow pace.

These were certainly some of the reasons why John Fitch, of Windsor, Connecticut, set out to build a passenger-carrying steamboat in 1785.

John Fitch was not the only man who saw a future in steamboats. James Rumsey, a Virginian, William Henry, a Pennsylvanian and Samuel Morey, a Vermont Yankee, were among those who succeeded in building such vessels before 1790, but they did not make commercial successes of their boats, perhaps because it was difficult to raise money for projects which some people considered foolish. Even James Watt had little or no interest in having his steam engines used in boats.

John Fitch, though, had visions of steamboats that could ply up and down the great rivers of the West, where they should be in great demand by the pioneers. Fitch knew the West better than many, for he had trudged through the Ohio territory as a trader until he was captured by Indians, who destroyed everything he had, sparing his life to make him their captive and slave. Eventually he escaped from the Indian camp near Lake Erie and made his way more than 350 miles to a town north of Philadelphia where, in 1785, he built his first "side-wheeler" steamboat and tested it on the Schuylkill River.

The boat traveled slowly, but Fitch sought to improve it by doing away with the paddle wheel at the side and rigging a high framework to which twelve long oars were attached vertically—six on a side. A connection between the engine and the oars caused them to dip in and out of the water, much in the way we paddle a canoe. These were not satisfactory, so Fitch kept experimenting, building a total of five vessels.

In 1788 he finally obtained a patent for a steamboat driven by a paddle wheel at the stern, but he had spent most of his money for his materials and tests. Still convinced that his invention could revolutionize transportation, Fitch tried in vain to get financial backing for it. He even pleaded with Benjamin Franklin to seek government support for the steamboat, but Franklin refused. Noting Fitch's shabby clothes, Franklin offered him money as charity, and Fitch stormed out indignantly.

In visit after visit he plagued members of the state legislatures of New York, New Jersey and Virginia for help, and although he failed to get any financial aid he did obtain an agreement whereby he alone could operate steam-driven vessels in the waters controlled by those three states.

Under this agreement, from June 14 to September 10, 1790, John Fitch operated a steam ferry on a fairly regular schedule between Philadelphia, Pennsylvania, and Burlington, New Jersey, on the Delaware River. Speed: four miles an hour, later increased to eight. Still unable to find backers who would put up money to build improved boats, Fitch went to France hoping that people there would share his optimism about progress in transportation, but the French were no more sympathetic than the Americans.

During his stay in France, Fitch lent his steamboat plans to the American consul, who might be able to find some interested parties. The consul failed to do so, but he did show Fitch's plans to another American, Robert Fulton, who was conducting experiments on a submarine which he hoped to sell to the French government.

Discouraged and unhappy, John Fitch returned to America only to find himself in more trouble. The navigation rights granted to him had expired and were not renewed. James Rumsey, the Virginia inventor, claimed that Fitch had stolen some of his ideas, and court battles began. In despair Fitch finally went to Bardstown, Kentucky, where he owned some land, and made one more valiant effort to interest Kentuckians in his ideas. When he failed he failed completely.

He offered to give his landlord three hundred acres of

Fitch-owned land if the landlord would keep him supplied with whiskey for the rest of Fitch's life.

The landlord agreed, and Fitch did nothing but drink. He lost weight, his shabby clothes hung on his body like rags on a scarecrow, and he had no interest in himself or his surroundings. In July, 1798, he killed himself, apparently by taking a dose of opium, and was buried in an unmarked grave in the public burying ground. (His grave was not discovered until 1855.)

In the year Fitch died, 1798, Robert R. Livingston, one of America's wealthiest men, applied for and was given the navigation rights that were originally granted to John Fitch—but with the understanding that within one year he would produce a steamboat with a speed of at least four miles an hour.

To build the boat, Livingston worked with Nicholas J. Roosevelt and Colonel John Stevens, the latter an inventor in his own right. Stevens, who was familiar with Watt's steam engine and who had seen John Fitch's steamboat in operation, built a boat in 1798 that sailed on the Hudson River; but it failed to make a speed of four miles an hour, and the rights that were granted to Livingston were revoked after the twelve-month period.

Colonel Stevens was destined to make real contributions to America's progress in transportation, but not until a few years later.

In 1801 Robert Livingston became American minister to France. There he met Robert Fulton, an artist who had come to Europe to study with the famous Benjamin West. In England young Fulton was commissioned to paint the portrait of the Earl of Devon, and during this project he met several engineers who were the earl's friends. In discussing their various accomplishments Fulton became more interested in engineering and inventions than in art, and he created some devices of his own, including a way to raise canal boats on inclined ramps rather than by water-filled locks.

Fulton did considerable work to invent a submarine and torpedo, and although he demonstrated its military value he failed to sell it to the French government. He continued, however, to be interested in steam as a driving force.

When he met Robert Livingston the subject of steamboats was of mutual interest, and it was agreed that Livingston would provide money for Fulton to experiment with the building of a steam-driven surface vessel.

At about this time an Englishman named William Symington built a steamboat, the *Charlotte Dundas*, on which a paddle wheel at the stern was driven by a steam engine made by Watt & Boulton. Although it was eventually abandoned, it did work satisfactorily for a time, and Robert Fulton studied its operation as it sailed the River Clyde.

In 1802 and 1803 Fulton built two boats which were tried on the Seine River in France. One sank and the other was so heavy that its engine barely moved it. Fulton decided to continue his work in the United States, so he ordered a large steam engine from Watt & Boulton to be shipped to America, and in 1806 Fulton himself returned home and began work on a new steamboat.

As the vessel's framework took shape, people laughed at Fulton for even thinking that such a huge boat might move without sails. The craft was 133 feet long, 7 feet deep, 18 feet wide, and when completed weighed 160 tons. Its paddle wheels were 15 feet in diameter and 4 feet wide. How could any steam engine possibly move such a monster through the water? To the public it became "Fulton's Folly."

To Fulton and Livingston the boat was the *Clermont*,

named for Livingston's Hudson River estate. When the New York newspapers announced that the *Clermont* would leave Cortlandt Street "at six and a half o'clock on Friday morning, the fourth of August [1807]," to carry passengers up the Hudson to Albany, readers shook their heads and asked, "Do you think anyone will be fool enough to go?"

According to one eyewitness account, an elderly man was overheard talking to a youth who was to make the journey. "John," the older one said, "will thee risk thy life in such a concern? I tell thee she is the most fearful wild fowl living, and thy father ought to restrain thee!"

On that historic Friday morning it seemed that almost everyone in New York came to watch the departure—or disaster. Thousands of men, women and children crowded the docks, the roofs, the windows of water-front buildings and any other vantage points. Many expected to see the vessel explode, and indeed its appearance was not one to inspire confidence.

All machinery was in plain sight, without housing of any kind. A forward deck provided some shelter for the crew. At the stern, directly in front of the helmsman, was the entrance to the passenger cabin, which contained twelve berths.

The engine was fueled with pine logs to get up steam. Clouds of black smoke belched from the tall iron chimney, and tongues of steam hissed out of tiny crevices and valves of the engine.

Spectators laughed and cheered and yelled. "Don't forget your oars!" one man cried.

"And don't forget your prayers!" called another.

"It's a long swim to Albany!" a woman shouted.

"Give our regards to the fishes!"

Robert Fulton smiled as he paced the deck, confident that

the jeers would turn to cheers once the boat was under way. At his signal the engine began to clank and the huge paddle wheels splashed and churned the water. Slowly the *Clermont* steamed into the open river and headed north, and within a few moments a tremendous cheer welled up from ten thousand throats ashore. It was echoed by happy shouts from the intrepid passengers. The fare for the trip was seven dollars, and most of the riders felt that they had already received their money's worth in thrills.

As the *Clermont* sailed past West Point the entire garrison turned out to watch and cheer. At every settlement along the way people came to the river banks to see this strange new creation. Many who lived near the river and had not known of the voyage were startled and frightened by the clanking of the machinery, the billowing smoke and the splashing of the paddle wheels. Families in small sailboats and rowboats came out to get a closer look. A ferryboat at Fishkill was crowded with women, all waving handkerchiefs.

"That's the finest sight we've seen yet!" Fulton said.

As it churned upriver at night the *Clermont* scared many country folk who heard the splash of the wheels and saw showers of sparks streaming like fireworks from the smokestack. Few passengers slept, because the excitement of the trip kept them wide awake.

Early the next afternoon the *Clermont* arrived at Livingston's estate, 110 miles from New York, and stayed there overnight. The following day it completed the voyage to Albany, having traveled the entire 150 miles upstream in thirty-two hours. The return trip downstream was made in thirty hours.

Fulton built housings for the machinery and paddle wheels, partitioned cabins and made other improvements, then began regular trips to Albany and back, often carrying a hundred passengers. The journeys had to be discontinued when the river froze in winter, but the day of the steamboat had arrived.

It was also in 1807 that Colonel John Stevens built a steam-propelled side-wheeler, the *Phoenix*. Since Fulton and Livingston had exclusive rights to navigate the Hudson, Stevens decided to take his vessel to Philadelphia; and in 1808 the *Phoenix*, under command of the colonel's son, Robert, sailed out of New York Harbor and into the open sea. She reached Philadelphia safely, and for more than five years made regular round trips between Philadelphia and Trenton, New Jersey. Of great importance was the fact that this was the first ocean-going steamboat, the vanguard of other vessels that were to be not only infinitely more powerful but also much greater in size, leading to the ocean liners of our own time which are self-contained floating cities.

These men—Evans, Fitch, Stevens, Fulton and others—gave a substantial push to the Industrial Revolution by their development of improved water transportation. Trade and commerce increased because both manufacturers and farmers could now ship factory goods and foodstuffs more readily. People, too, could and did travel by boat to build homes and towns in what was wild and lonely land.

There were disadvantages, however. Boats were fine for hauling goods and carrying passengers, but they had to float and the navigable waterways did not reach the places where many people wanted to settle in the interior. Man-made waterways would have to be carved out of the earth if boats were to operate away from the rivers and lakes and oceans.

More and better roads were needed, too, so that people and products could reach areas where boats could never go.

CHAPTER 5

Live Mules and Iron Horses

On a bright October day in 1834 a flatboat pulled into the canal landing at Hollidaysburg, Pennsylvania. Aboard were Jesse Chrisman, his wife and children, and all of their household belongings, together with a few pigs and pigeons. The Chrismans had left their farm on the Juniata River to join the growing migration to the West, and were heading for Illinois.

At the Hollidaysburg landing young Jesse tried to sell his flatboat, named the *Hit or Miss*, expecting that it could take him no farther West. His sales efforts were overheard by a representative of The Portage Railroad Company, who made a novel suggestion.

"We might be able to carry your boat over the mountain on a railroad car," the man said.

It was true that passengers on their way to Pittsburgh changed at Hollidaysburg from canal boats to railroad cars which were pulled by a stationary engine to the Allegheny mountaintop, 2500 feet high, then lowered down the other side where they could board a canal boat at Johnstown and finish the journey to Pittsburgh by water. But no one yet had hauled a flatboat over the mountain.

Husky men and horses dragged the vessel from the river to the railroad tracks, lifted it onto a flatcar and tied it with ropes. The climb was slow, for the vessel was heavy, and the railroad manager ordered his men to proceed with caution. The Chrisman family sat aboard the boat as it made its way up five inclined slopes. In the afternoon they had lunch aboard the boat, and soon after sunset they reached the mountaintop, where it was decided to stay until morning.

There the *Hit or Miss* with its human cargo and its pigs and pigeons stayed under the stars, like Noah's Ark on Mount Ararat. At dawn the descent began, and in a few hours the flatboat was placed in the canal at Johnstown. It carried the Chrismans safely to Pittsburgh and eventually down the Ohio River to St. Louis, not far from their new home.

Probably this was the first time a boat had sailed over a mountain!

In the eighteenth century there were no roads as we know them today. People who walked from one place to another usually followed trails made by animals or Indians, or made new paths through primeval forests and across open meadows. In the early nineteenth century, settlers built their homes and villages near the ocean or close to rivers and lakes, because it was much easier to transport people and goods in canoes, boats and sailing ships than in land vehicles.

After the American Revolution this was still primarily an agricultural nation. In 1803 the Louisiana Purchase added an area of almost 828,000 square miles to the United States. Soon these vast lands of the Ohio and Mississippi Valleys were opened to settlement, and thousands of people left the East to stake out farms on fertile land that was practically free for the asking. They rode horseback, they walked, they traveled in canvas-covered Conestoga wagons drawn by oxen or mules, lumbering through mountain passes, crossing swift rivers, fighting Indians, sickness, weariness and despair.

As these pioneers settled in the new land and built up their farms and homes, many learned that it was useless to grow huge crops of wheat, corn and barley or to raise big herds of cattle or sheep because it was too difficult to take their grain and livestock to market. Those who lived near rivers or the Great Lakes could use the water roads, but even then it was a long, long journey down the Mississippi to the Gulf of Mexico and by ship around Florida to New York, Boston and other East Coast market centers. And many farmers who lived inland were compelled to raise only what their own families could use or what they might sell locally.

Some formed caravans of horses and mules to carry goods across the Allegheny Mountains. A caravan might comprise forty or fifty pack animals, each with its head tied to the tail of the one in front, each loaded with grain, whiskey, flour, fruit and pigs or chickens, bound for eastern markets. Returning, the pack train carried salt, cotton, iron or other goods to be used by the frontier families.

Separated from the centers of population and the comforts of city living, wringing a livelihood from what had been a wilderness, and having other common interests in farming and cattle-raising, the settlers developed a democratic spirit which was completely different from the aristocratic ways of the coastal areas. As their numbers increased they also represented a growing new political influence with strong sectional leanings, and it became more and more evident that improvements must be made in methods of transportation if all parts of the expanding country were to be linked together as a union.

Besides, the importers and manufacturers in the population centers needed more customers to buy their products, and their businesses could not grow very fast until ways were found to bring sellers and buyers together more easily. Growing numbers of settlers were flocking into western lands, and the need to get their produce and livestock to market became increasingly urgent. In short, both industry and agriculture could expand and prosper when good roads made better transportation possible.

Trails between towns became rough wagon roads, but they were ribbons of dust in dry weather and mudholes when it rained. It was not unusual for horses to sink belly-deep in soupy mud, and carriages and stagecoaches often overturned, causing injuries to passengers.

At best it still took travelers from New York City three days to go overland to Philadelphia, six days to Boston, six weeks to St. Louis, often jouncing over rutty roads in heavy wagons or uncomfortable stagecoaches.

As the westward expansion increased, so did complaints from the settlers, who kept clamoring for better roads. Some cities, including Boston and New York, "paved" certain main streets with cobblestones, later with wooden blocks and bricks, but these were luxuries unheard of in the interior.

One of the first serviceable roads in the United States was built from Lancaster to Philadelphia, Pennsylvania, in 1794. It was topped with stone and it made stagecoach travel reasonably safe and fairly comfortable over its sixty-nine-mile length. It also marked the beginning of a roadbuilding program that would one day have a tremendous effect upon the growth of American transportation and commerce.

In 1808, the year after the successful maiden voyage of Fulton's *Clermont*, work was begun on the building of a cross-country road to be known at the National Pike (now identified as Highway U. S. 40). As the new road inched westward toward Cumberland, Maryland, its progress was interrupted by the roar of British cannon and the answering thunder of American guns. The War of 1812 made national defense more important than highway construction, so picks and shovels yielded to swords and rifles.

Before the War of 1812 the "factory system" had not yet taken a good hold in the United States, and Americans still depended largely upon England for many imported goods. At the same time they exported iron, tobacco, farm products and livestock to Europe, so that there was a steady two-way commerce between the Old World and the New, and a good balance of trade.

At the outbreak of war this overseas business was halted by an embargo. Men whose profits had come from imports and exports were in danger of failing in business and sought desperately to find other ways to keep from going broke. With imports cut off, the United States needed its own sources of manufactured goods, so the capitalists invested money in new factories, partly as a patriotic duty, largely for their own profit. New textile mills were built and up went the production of cloth. Iron that would have been exported in peacetime was fashioned into farm implements, weapons and other products for home use. Shoes and other leather goods increased in quantity. Paper mills sprang up in New England, and forests were stripped to get pulpwood for papermaking. Coal from Pennsylvania mines came into greater use to provide power for mills not located on rivers and streams, and American ships formerly bound for English ports now plied up and down the East Coast carrying all manner of merchandise from state to coastal state.

To supply the North's demand for yarn, the southern plant·ers expanded their cotton fields, brought in more slaves when they could get them, and spent thousands of dollars to buy goods made in northern factories. Sheep-raisers, too, profited by the demand for wool and bought manufactured products.

All of this activity had important effects. Americans had won political independence from England in the Revolutionary War but had continued to depend economically upon Britain and other European countries until the War of 1812 virtually compelled them to be self-sufficient. Sectional differences grew stronger. The agricultural South promoted the growth and use of cotton, tobacco, rice and sugar cane. The industrial North was concerned primarily with manufacturing, and the growing West was becoming the nation's breadbasket, filled with cattle, wheat and other food products.

When the War of 1812 ended, foreign trade began again and new tariffs were imposed to keep down foreign competition and protect American manufacturers. Although overseas commerce was important, President James Madison in 1815 recommended, among other things, a national network of roads and canals that would tie the country together. With the approval of Congress work was resumed on the National Pike, and by 1818 it stretched as far West as Wheeling, West Virginia. It was, of course, a dirt road and not paved as it is today.

Work began on turnpikes in other areas, and throughout the 1820s men hacked away trees and brush and built roads connecting various parts of the Midwest with the East Coast and Gulf of Mexico. The roads were crude and often impassable, but they were better than no roads at all.

In the early 1830s, when good roads were still few and steamboats were built in growing numbers, there was a public clamor for canals to connect roads, rivers, lakes and ocean. A canal—the first one in the United States—had been completed

in 1793. It permitted boats to avoid the rapids of the Connecticut River at South Hadley, Massachusetts, by floating them in
large tanks which were then hauled by water power over two
levels to quiet water. Another was built in 1800 in the southeastern part of South Carolina and connected the Santee River
with the Cooper River, which flowed into Charleston Harbor.
This was the Santee Canal, probably the first true canal in this
country.

The real canal-building era began when DeWitt Clinton,
governor of New York in 1817, led a state-sponsored project
to build a canal from the Hudson River at Troy, New York,
to Buffalo on Lake Erie. The 363-mile ditch was completed
in 1825 and the famous Erie Canal was in business. This water
road was of tremendous importance because it not only provided a good route from East to West, but also reduced the
time and costs of carrying goods in both directions. According to one historian, before the canal was built a New York
manufacturer had to pay one hundred dollars a ton for freight
carried overland to Buffalo, and the trip took twenty days.
By canal boat this cost soon dropped to three dollars a ton,
and the journey was made in one week.

The Erie Canal was a construction feat that established civil
engineering as a worthy profession, but most significant was
the simplified transportation that enabled thousands of families
from coastal areas to float to the Great Lakes country and beyond to claim new lands and begin new lives.

The Erie Canal and another connecting Albany, New York,
with Lake Champlain were financial successes, and land along
the routes skyrocketed in price. When other states saw the
profits rolling into New York's treasury there was a scramble
to build new canals in other places. Another reason was that

the Erie Canal was diverting considerable trade from states such as Pennsylvania, Maryland, Delaware and New Jersey. Within a few years there were canals in Massachusetts, Connecticut, New Jersey, Maryland, across the whole state of Pennsylvania, and in Virginia, Ohio, Indiana, Illinois and Michigan; and the population of these states began to boom. Still in existence, though no longer used for hauling freight, is the Chesapeake and Ohio Canal, which extends from Washington, D. C., to Cumberland, Maryland.

A Maryland resident, Mrs. Edith Martin Armstrong, in 1947 explored the history of part of this canal and Cabin John Park, a few miles outside the District of Columbia. Her findings included this bit of Americana:

The canal was as fascinating as it was annoying. Many a night residents of the neighborhood were awakened by a boatman warning the lock-tender of his approach. There was a bell system between the locks, but at night it often failed to arouse the lock-tender. Consequently a weird "Hoo-wee!" or a lusty "Hey, lock!" or a few notes or a tune on a horn, broke the silence of the night. Lights from swinging lanterns were visible. Then there was an impatient yell at the mules as the water rushed to fill or empty the lock.

On summer evenings many watched the boats locked through and marveled at the homey scenes that represented life on a canal boat. Often a mother rocked and sang to her baby, the wash hanging from a pulley line above the boat. Children romped about the boat tied to a rope and occasionally one hung over the side, crying lustily to be pulled back on deck. Sometimes the woman aboard handled the rudder, which taxed even a man's strength to keep the boat from hitting the bank. Usually the men drove the mules along the towpath, either walking beside them or riding on their backs. Then again, a youngster or perhaps the women aboard would take a turn. Two mules enjoyed stable life while two, three or four trudged the towpath.

The canal-building era and the steamboat brought a decline in the building of roads, and by 1840 there were about four thousand miles of canals in the country.

There was one big obstacle to canal travel—the weather. For about four months every year the man-made waterways in the north country were frozen solid, and canal, river and lake travel came to a standstill. Just as steamboats and canal boats had offered advantages over the muddy roads and lumbering wagons, so now did another form of transportation outshine both and give a tremendous boost to settlement, agriculture and industry. This was the era of the "iron horse"—the steam locomotive and the railroad.

Oliver Evans, with his strange *Oruktor Amphibolos*, had shown that steam could power vehicles on land and predicted the coming of carriages that would run on "two sets of railways." Evans himself never built a railway carriage, but in 1804, the very year in which the *Oruktor Amphibolos* made its bow, an Englishman named Richard Trevithick designed and built a steam-driven locomotive that hauled carts loaded with iron ore over a set of tracks in Wales. It is said that Trevithick had seen Evans' patent drawings and patterned his steam engine after Evans' own design.

In 1811 another Englishman, John Blenkinsop, built a steam locomotive which was used for several years to haul heavy loads of coal.

It remained for a third Britisher, George Stephenson, to open the way for the real development of rail travel. He was born June 9, 1781, to a poverty-stricken family near Newcastle-on-Tyne, and as a young boy he was compelled to work in the Killingworth coal mines where his father struggled to eke out a living. He had virtually no education, and even when he was eighteen years old he was unable to read or write.

At the coal mine he was assigned to attend a pump powered by one of James Watt's steam engines. He studied the engine part by part and was eager to learn more about such machines, but that was something that required the reading of books, and Stephenson couldn't read.

One of his neighbors was a schoolteacher, and in response to Stephenson's plea he agreed to teach the boy his "letters." Night after night Stephenson did his homework, practicing constantly, until he was able to read technical books. Then all of his spare time was devoted to studying books about steam power, occasionally seeking advice from his teacher about passages that were not quite clear.

One day the pump at the mine broke down. The experienced mechanics called upon to fix it were powerless to find and correct the trouble, and at Stephenson's request the mineowners gave him permission to try his hand at repairs. He dismantled the pump completely, checked and cleaned each part, made a few minor adjustments and within four days had it reassembled and running perfectly. The delighted owners paid him a reward of ten pounds and promoted him to the job of "engineer."

In 1813 Stephenson saw the Blenkinsop locomotive and decided that he could build a better one. He persuaded the mineowners to back him in building a locomotive to haul coal on rails from the mine to a shipping port nine miles away. He completed the engine, named the "Blücher," in 1814, and used it to pull thirty tons of coal in eight cars over a steep grade at a speed of about four miles an hour.

Stephenson later engineered the Stockton & Darlington Railroad and the Liverpool & Manchester Railroad, and built a prize-winning locomotive known as "The Rocket." When he died in 1848 he was worth a fortune and had lived to see the enormous contribution his knowledge and inventions had made to industrial progress.

In 1815, when George Stephenson's "Blücher" was hauling coal from the Killingworth Colliery, Colonel John Stevens of Hoboken, New Jersey, obtained a state charter for the operation of a steam railroad between the Delaware and Raritan Rivers. Stevens, whose side-wheeler, the *Phoenix*, had made the first steam-powered ocean voyage, had long been confident that steam-driven locomotives would be even more effective on land than steamboats were on water.

His charter was never used, for the proposed Delaware-Raritan Railroad was never built. John Stevens, however, experimented for years in the building of locomotives, and by 1825 he had built one which ran on a half-mile circular railway track on the lower lawn of his Hoboken estate. While this could hardly be called a railroad, Stevens' locomotive was the first to travel on rails in America. (A small model of the locomotive, and the boiler and safety valve used on the original, are now in The Smithsonian Institution in Washington, D. C.)

The first locomotive to operate in the United States on a railroad built for commercial traffic was the *Stourbridge Lion*, a British-made engine which arrived in New York City on May 13, 1829, and was put aboard the Hudson River steamboat *Congress* for delivery to the Delaware & Hudson Canal Company at Rondout, New York. It was not very satisfactory and did not stay long in service.

Real American railroading began in 1830 when the Baltimore & Ohio Railroad Company opened the first thirteen miles of a line whose owners planned to have it reach to Ohio. This was the first American railway to operate under a charter for the carrying of freight and passengers. For the first few months a B. & O. car was hauled on tracks by horses, but during the summer of 1830 it was decided to race the "old gray mare" against a steam locomotive.

The locomotive was the *Tom Thumb*, built by Peter Cooper, a New York inventor. Its boiler was made of rifle barrels, and its four wheels were only thirty inches in diameter. The *Tom Thumb* traveled the thirteen-mile track from Baltimore to Ellicott's Mills in a little more than an hour. The horse-drawn car was waiting at Ellicott's Mills to race on the return trip.

Probably most of the railroad officials and spectators were fairly sure that the steam engine would win the contest, but a race is never over until the finish line is crossed. For most of the way the *Tom Thumb* was out in front, hissing and puffing and billowing smoke. Nearing Baltimore, however, a belt drive on the engine began to slip. Steam pressure dropped rapidly, and in a few minutes the not-so-old gray mare strutted proudly past the mechanical monster and received a victor's reward of sugar lumps.

Despite the outcome of the race, B. & O. officials were convinced that steam locomotives were practicable and necessary for long hauls, and in 1831 they bought and operated the *York*, a three-and-a-half-ton engine with a top speed of thirty miles an hour.

The Baltimore & Ohio was not the first railroad to use a locomotive on a regularly scheduled run in the United States. That honor goes to the South Carolina Canal and Rail-Road Company, which made the first "official" trip with passengers on December 25, 1830. The locomotive was the *Best Friend of Charleston*, and it made the run out of Charleston over the company's six miles of track. By 1833 this railroad stretched from Charleston to Augusta, Georgia, and was then the longest continuous railway in the world.

The *Best Friend*, the *Stourbridge Lion*, the *Tom Thumb* and other early "iron horses" fired the imagination of more and more inventors, and bigger and better engines were designed and built. Many of the railroads covered fairly small areas and were dedicated to promoting local commercial interests, but as more lines came into existence there were consolidations and mergers that brought tracks and trains across large territories. Many were in areas where towns not yet in existence were expected. More people were traveling West, trade was increasing between East and West, and the frontier was being rolled back steadily. Railroads were civilizing the wilderness.

With the upturn in manufacturing and farming, great numbers of European immigrants crossed the seas to begin new lives in the United States, and the population mounted rapidly. Immigration caused new problems in industry. The newcomers from overseas were willing to work for wages lower than those paid to Americans, and in many places the immigrants were hired to replace American workers.

Many Europeans who migrated to America had lived in countries ruled by kings and nobles, and the American system of democratic government was both surprising and satisfying to the immigrants. They realized quickly that the economic life of the United States was governed by the capitalists, who supplied money for factory construction and the production of goods, and by the working men and women who produced the goods.

Both classes wanted a voice in government to protect their own interests, so both took active part to support the democracy and to make themselves an influence upon the governing bodies. New states were sending representatives and senators to Congress, political parties were divided on sectional issues, the farmers opposed the manufacturers (and vice versa), and there were differences about tariffs on imports, taxes, banking and other economic issues, just as there are today. People were becoming better informed on these subjects because improved transportation had provided faster and better communication among various parts of the country.

As the wilderness slowly gave way to civilization, stores opened for business, and there was an increased demand for food and supplies, which meant more work and more income for factory workers. Of course, some towns never grew and many storekeepers failed for lack of trade, especially in places far removed from rivers, canals or railroads; but the nation was on the move toward a future bound to be marked by multitudes of successes and failures in many fields of endeavor.

More ammunition for the Industrial Revolution was being produced by American inventors, many of whom would surely be amazed if they could see the results of their creative talents today.

CHAPTER 6

Three for the Money

A man's ability to remember details once again gave a healthy push to the Industrial Revolution when a young Boston merchant, Francis Cabot Lowell, traveled in Europe for his health. While visiting England in 1811 he was impressed by clothmakers at work on power looms, and as a shrewd businessman Lowell realized that such looms would be a tremendous boon to the textile industry in America.

The British, however, still prohibited the exportation of their textile machinery and Lowell was unable to take any with him to the United States. Just as Samuel Slater had done years earlier, he studied the design and operation of the power looms until he believed that he could duplicate one from memory. For assurance, however, he made a few sketches of parts of the machinery and succeeded in smuggling them out of England.

Lowell returned to Boston in 1813 and induced his brother-in-law, Patrick Jackson, to provide money for the building of a complete, modern mechanized textile factory, which was erected in Waltham, Massachusetts, on the banks of a stream that could provide water power.

Lowell made sketches from his recollected observations of the British machinery and took them, along with those he had smuggled out of England, to a friend, Paul Moody, an expert machinist. Together, Lowell and Moody drew plans for construction of the machinery and its installation in the Waltham mill, but in the planning stage they made changes which were improvements over some of the British creations.

Before the year 1813 ended, the machinery was completed and set up in the mill, which was chartered as a corporation under the name of the Boston Manufacturing Company. The machinery worked perfectly, and for the first time the United States had a textile factory in which all operations from cotton bale to finished cloth were not only mechanized but also performed under one roof.

At first business was rather poor because most people considered British textiles to be better than any thus far made in America, but the War of 1812 had stopped British imports and Americans were compelled to turn to domestic products. Gradually the word spread that the Lowell-Moody mill was producing cloth as good as, or maybe better than, the English fabrics, and Francis Cabot Lowell lived long enough to see his investment return a handsome profit. He died in 1817, but the business he built continued to thrive.

Sales increased to the point where the company had to expand. For lack of enough water power in Waltham the owners bought an abandoned canal which skirted a waterfall on the Merrimack River, and in 1822 organized a new corporation, the Merrimack Manufacturing Company, capable of producing thousands of yards of cloth each month and also of making calico prints.

This second factory was a big success, and the owners began to build more textile plants, engineered new canals and sold some of their land holdings. They founded a town which they named in honor of Francis Cabot Lowell, and they continued to build mills and hire scores of workers who came from other places to get jobs. By 1826 the textile manufacturing center of the nation was Lowell, Massachusetts.

Just as the growth of manufacturing was speeded up by new mechanical inventions, so was that of agriculture. Western farmers who were once quite isolated were getting better access to markets because of new roads, canals and even a few railroads, so they could now grow bigger crops for profit and not just for home use.

In the early 1830s, when the textile industry was thriving, the demand for wheat and other grains was met only by imports from abroad because the domestic crops were in short supply. Western farms were ideally suited to the growing of wheat. Both land and climate were excellent, and it would be relatively easy to plant and grow several thousand acres—but harvesting such an area would require the help of more men than there were crumbs in a bowl of biscuits.

Harvesting was strictly a hand operation. The wheat was reaped with a scythe, which was simply a long, slightly curved steel blade attached to a wooden handle. With wide, smooth strokes the farmer swung the scythe across the standing grain, making a path through the field as he trudged its length, while helpers (if he had any) picked up and bound the cut wheat.

A man who could reap more than one acre a day with the scythe was practically a champion, although there is a record of a Pennsylvanian who once cut twelve and a half acres of wheat in one day and virtually ruined his health.

Wheat farmers tried to help each other with harvests, but their crops all ripened at about the same time and if they did not reap their grain within a few days it would best be left standing as food for cattle. For this reason most wheat farmers raised only what they could use or what they knew they could harvest and sell locally.

The harvesting problem was solved by a father-and-son team and by another man who knew nothing of their work. The father and son were Robert and Cyrus McCormick of Rockbridge County, Virginia. The other man was Obed Hussey of Baltimore, Maryland.

Both the elder McCormick and Hussey were inventors. One story goes that Hussey was in Cincinnati, Ohio, creating a new kind of mold for making candles, when a friend ridiculed him.

"What are you wasting time on that thing for?" the friend asked. "Why don't you work on something worthwhile? Something big?"

Hussey grinned. "I'm satisfied."

"Satisfied! You're afraid."

"That so?" Hussey continued to smile. "What am I afraid of?"

"You're afraid to tackle a real problem—a big problem. You'd rather fool around with these—these doodads."

"What big problem did you have in mind?"

"Oh, any big problem. There are lots of them."

"Name one."

The friend was silent for a few moments, then said, "All right—why don't you make a harvesting machine?"

"A harvesting machine?"

"You know, for harvesting wheat. The farmers cut it by hand with scythes. They'd pay almost anything to get a machine that could do it."

"The English already have such machines," Hussey said.

"Yes, but they don't work well. What we need is one that is dependable and efficient. It would be worth a fortune."

Hussey was thoughtful. "I suppose it would," he said.

"Then why don't you try it?"

The inventor said, "I've got to finish this candle mold, then maybe I'll think about it some."

Hussey not only thought about it, but also worked on it. He improved upon a principle discovered and used by Patrick Bell, a Scottish minister, in which a series of overlapping blades worked like shears to cut off grain close to the ground. The shears were attached to a long bar at one side of a horse-drawn two-wheeled rig on which the farmer sat as he drove through his wheat field. The cut grain fell on a platform behind the shears and was raked off by the farmer, to be gathered up from the field.

In 1831, while Hussey was at work on his invention, twenty-two-year-old Cyrus McCormick was also experimenting with a harvesting machine. His father, Robert, had tried for several years to build a mechanical device that would duplicate the actions of a man swinging a scythe, but his efforts had all failed and he turned his attention to other projects. Young Cyrus, however, had watched and helped his father, and was determined to try his own hand at building a successful reaper.

His first working model was completed in 1831, and he obtained permission to try it on a stand of wheat owned by Farmer Ruff of Steele's Tavern, some miles west of Charlottesville, Virginia. McCormick's crude contraption was drawn by four horses, and as he started them around the field there was a chorus of boos, jeers and laughter from a group of farm hands who feared that the machine, if successful, would throw them out of work.

The field was rough and somewhat rocky, and the reaper shook and rattled as it cut through the grain. Farmer Ruff, walking in the machine's wake, saw that it left a ragged stubble, tore many heads from the wheat, and threatened to ruin his entire crop. He ran up and halted the horses.

"Stop!" he shouted. "Stop this thing right now!"

McCormick was puzzled. "What is it? What's the matter?"

"The matter is that you're chewing my wheat to pieces, you and your foolishness. Now you get this thing out of here and keep it out! You hear me?"

Young Cyrus drove off the field, half angry, half discouraged, yet convinced that his idea would work. Another farmer who had witnessed the demonstration apparently shared McCormick's confidence, for he invited him to try the reaper on his wheat.

The next morning McCormick accepted the invitation and harvested six acres of grain during that day, the equivalent of the work of six men with scythes.

It appears that both Obed Hussey and Cyrus Hall McCormick deserve credit for the success of the reaper. Hussey patented his machine in 1833 and became widely known as "The Man Who Made Bread Cheap." McCormick's patent was issued in 1834. McCormick proved to be the better businessman, for he continued to improve his reaper, founded the International Harvester Company and became a millionaire before he died in 1884. Hussey, on the other hand, continued to make and sell reapers, but he refused to use other men's inventions to make his machine more efficient. Gradually his business declined and he finally sold it for $200,000. He then turned to the design and manufacture of steam-driven plows.

The reaper revolutionized American agriculture and was an immense boon to manufacturing as well. Bigger farm crops meant bigger income for farmers, who bought more manufactured goods. Mechanized farms and mechanized factories began to change the lives and customs of people in all parts of the land, and although they did not see themselves in the midst of anything with such a fancy name as the "Industrial Revolution," they were aware that they were caught up in a whirl of progress and rapid change. Craftsmen who produced hand-made goods were gradually compelled to learn new manufacturing methods. As new factories were built, many farmers, especially in New England, gave up agriculture to work in the mills for steady pay. Since the factories increased the demand for cotton and wool, the southern plantation owners grew more crops and western sheep ranchers raised more livestock.

Thanks to Cyrus McCormick, men with mighty muscles and the stamina to wield a scythe while dripping sweat for twelve hours in the fields could be replaced if necessary by scrawny fellows riding above a clattering array of gears, belts, levers and blades, all designed to harvest crops more quickly and more easily than squads of farmers on foot.

Giants were no more courageous than a nineteenth-century American named Charles Goodyear, although they were undoubtedly much stronger and in far better health. What Goodyear lacked in physical perfection was more than offset by his perseverance and faith.

Goodyear was born in 1800 in New Haven, Connecticut, where his father, Amasa, manufactured spoons, buttons, scythes and other products, including an invention of his own —the first steel pitchfork.

As a teen-ager Charles Goodyear landed a job in a hardware store in Philadelphia, where he worked until he was twenty-one, when he returned to New Haven and went into partnership with his father. Four years later he married and decided to go into business on his own. He gathered together many of the products made by his father, along with some other American-made goods, took them to Philadelphia and opened a hardware store.

The store was not a success, and Goodyear found a great deal of leisure time, which he devoted to reading and experimenting with new ideas in the hardware line. One of these was a metal valve designed for use in rubber life preservers, and in 1834, in an effort to sell it, Goodyear took the valve to the Roxbury India Rubber Company in New York City, which made and sold not only life preservers but also other goods made of rubber.

He was shocked to discover that the store was on the verge of going out of business. Its stock of rubber coats, rubber hats, rubber shoes and other rubber goods had melted in the summer heat and oozed into sticky, shapeless blobs. The distraught manager thought Goodyear's valve had possibilities, but obviously the store was not interested in buying it.

Charles Goodyear knew little about the "gum elastic" which in 1770 the British chemist Joseph Priestley had called "rubber" because he discovered that it could be used to rub out pencil marks on paper. People who had bought goods made of rubber found not only that heat decomposed and melted it, but also that cold made it so stiff and brittle that it broke quicker than boardinghouse dishes. Daniel Webster, for example, who later acted as Goodyear's attorney, told of his personal experience with the material.

"A friend in New York sent me a very fine cloak of India rubber and a hat of the same material," he said. "I did not succeed very well with them. I took the cloak one day and set it out in the cold. It stood very well by itself! I surmounted it with the hat, and many persons passing by supposed they saw standing on my porch the Farmer of Marshfield!"

Goodyear proposed to learn how to produce rubber that

wouldn't be affected by heat or cold, but he was to have a bitter uphill struggle. His hardware business failed and he was sent to debtor's prison, where he continued to experiment with raw rubber brought to him by his wife. His release from jail was the first of many, for he was destined to be in and out of debtors' prisons many times in the next ten years, but he never wavered in his purpose.

All his waking hours were spent on his experiments. When neighbors objected to the smell of fumes from his chemicals he went to New York to continue his work. There he became so ill that his friends and family begged him to return to New Haven, which he did, but he refused to give up his search.

In 1836 Goodyear found that sulfur seemed to "cure" rubber in such a way that the rubber would not be affected by climate. He was so convinced of this that he persuaded the federal government to award him a contract for mail sacks made from his new formula. He made scores of the mailbags, but by the time the order was to be delivered the rubber had begun to deteriorate internally and when the heavy sacks were lifted the handles tore away. The sulfur had affected the rubber as Goodyear thought, but the "curing" was only on the surface and not throughout the material.

After his failure with the mailbag contract Goodyear's friends deserted him completely. He was an idiot, a fool, a lunatic, a dreamer. Indeed, some of his actions seemed to support these epithets. He made and wore a suit made entirely of rubber. According to one story, a stranger in town asked a local man how he could recognize Goodyear.

"That's easy," the local man answered. "If you see a man wearing an India rubber coat, cap, stockings, vest and shoes, and carrying an India rubber purse without a penny in it, that's Goodyear."

Penniless though he was, Goodyear managed to continue his work in the home of his brother-in-law in Woburn, Massachusetts.

Seeking a way to make sulfur "cure" all parts of the rubber, he boiled a mixture of the two on the kitchen stove. As he ladled out the boiled goo, some of it overflowed to the top of the hot stove and sizzled and fried like a pancake. Goodyear scraped it off to throw away, but he noticed that the terrific heat had apparently not hardened the mixture. On the contrary, the piece was soft and pliable. This was difficult to understand, since heat had been the ruin of the whole rubber business.

Excited by his accidental discovery, Goodyear nailed the cooked blob to the house outside the front door. The date was February 23, 1839. It was very cold, and if by morning the specimen was hard and brittle it would represent just another disappointment.

The next morning Goodyear's heart must have thumped as he opened the door to get his fried discovery. What a thrill must have surged through his body as his trembling fingers touched the blob and squeezed it and found it to be still soft and flexible! Five years of poverty, misery, sickness, hope, despair and struggle were climaxed by an accidental miracle.

Ironically, intense heat had transformed rubber into a material that could withstand its greatest enemy—heat. Because of the part played by fire in his discovery, Goodyear called the process "vulcanization" after Vulcan, the Roman god of fire.

Goodyear's happiness and excitement were shared by his wife and children, who had borne their own share of suffering, but if he believed that his troubles were over he was soon disillusioned. The public had learned by bitter experience that rubber products were ruined by hot and cold weather. Manufacturers of rubber goods had lost fortunes. People were unwilling to believe that Goodyear's discovery made rubber any more practicable than it used to be. His hard-won success threatened to be a failure.

Although plagued by stomach pains and crippled by gout, during the next five long years Goodyear not only worked out improvements in his process, but also limped through the hills and valleys of New England searching for someone to give him financial backing for the manufacture of his vulcanized rubber. His efforts were in vain until 1844, when he obtained a patent for his process.

When news of the patent spread through the commercial world, unscrupulous men pirated Goodyear's idea, while others cheated him out of a fortune by paying him ridiculously low royalties for his process. Goodyear himself seemed more interested in the possible uses of rubber than in money, but the infringements of his patent and the unfounded attacks on his rights made him a reluctant contender in several court fights. In 1852 the showdown came in the U. S. Circuit Court in Trenton, New Jersey, where the then Secretary of State, the famous Daniel Webster, acted as Goodyear's attorney.

In his plea Webster demanded to know if any man in the world had discovered the vulcanizing process before Goodyear. If so, Webster asked, "Who is he? Where is he? On what continent does he live? Who has heard of him? What books treat of him? What man among all the men on earth has seen him, known him or named him? Yet it is certain that this discovery has been made. It is certain that it exists. . . . It is a matter of common knowledge all over the civilized world. . . . It is certain that this curious result has grown into knowledge by somebody's discovery and invention. And who is that somebody? . . . . If Charles Goodyear did not make this discovery, who did make it? Who did make it? . . . . We want to know the name, and the habitation, and the location of the man upon the face of this globe who invented vulcanized rubber, if it be not he who now sits before us!"

The court found in Goodyear's behalf, settling once and for all his claim as the original inventor of the vulcanization process.

Although Goodyear died owing some $200,000, he held no resentment toward the world. In a book printed on rubber sheets and bound with a rubber cover, he wrote: "The advantages of a career in life should not be estimated exclusively by the standard of dollars and cents, as is too often done. Man has just cause for regret when he sows and no one reaps."

The whole world reaped benefits from Goodyear's discovery, and also from Lowell's power loom and McCormick's reaper—three big contributions to the Industrial Revolution.

The factories that were built in the wake of these and other inventions needed workers, and hundreds of men and women left their farms to take jobs in industry. They built their houses near the factories, the growing communities attracted grocers, clothiers and other merchants who built stores, and in this way villages became towns and towns grew into great cities.

With this growth came community needs and problems such as sanitation, water supplies, municipal taxes, crime, law enforcement, housing, schools, transportation, recreation facilities and local government.

In many factory towns workers originally built houses and tenements close together and close to the factories where they were employed. Smoke and soot from industrial chimneys covered the outside of many such homes and darkened the interiors with a murky film of grime. Families grew, but living quarters often didn't, and crowded conditions along with property neglect in cities created depressed areas called "slums," accompanied by health hazards, immorality, delinquency and discord.

Along with the good and the bad, industrial America continued to move forward, and some of the most important inventions of all were on the way.

CHAPTER 7

Switches and Stitches

Charles Goodyear's discovery of the vulcanizing process was accidental, and history shows that other significant contributions to the Industrial Revolution grew from accidents.

According to one account an Italian lady, a common cold and a few dead frogs in 1790 led to new knowledge about electricity, a little-known force that was destined to take the Industrial Revolution out of the Water-, Horse- and Steam-Power Age and whisk it into high gear.

The story says that Mrs. Luigi Galvani of Bologna, Italy, whose husband was a professor of anatomy, contracted a cold and was treated by a doctor who prescribed a diet of frog broth. Servants caught several frogs, skinned and washed them, and left them on a table in the professor's laboratory. One of his assistants "who was conducting experiments with a large electrical machine which stood upon the same table, had occasion to draw sparks from the machine, and Galvani's wife, who was present, was surprised to observe that every time he did so the limbs of the dead frogs moved as if alive. She immediately communicated this strange incident to her husband, who repeated the experiment with the same result."

Continuing, the story adds, "Greatly struck by the phe-
nomenon, he determined to follow it up and henceforth devoted himself to experiments on the electricity of animals with
such zeal that, it is said, he became the terror of every frog
pond near Bologna. Another fortunate chance discovery re-
warded his perseverance. Having prepared the hinder parts of
several frogs for anatomical investigation, he passed copper
hooks through part of the dorsal parts, which remained above
the junction of the thighs, for the convenience of hanging
them up till they might be required for the purpose of experiment. In this manner he happened to suspend several upon the
iron balcony in front of his laboratory, when, to his inexpres-
sible astonishment, the limbs were thrown into strong convul-
sions."

Galvani called this effect "animal electricity," but another
Italian, Alessandro Volta, found that the phenomena was due
to a chemical reaction between iron and copper. Based upon
this finding Volta assembled a stack of disks of copper, zinc
and wet paper in alternate layers and proved that this combination generated an electric current. The stack became
known as the "Voltaic pile." This and more discoveries by
such pioneers as Hans Oersted, Sir Humphry Davy, Michael
Faraday, Georg S. Ohm and others across the seas added a new
and vital booster to the Industrial Revolution in America. This
addition was swift communication.

Communication and transportation in the United States
were virtually synonymous during the early years of the nineteenth century. Settlers who trudged westward on foot, or
drove horse- or ox-drawn carts over the mountains and plains,
were for a long time the only communication link between
the populated East and the advancing western frontier.

The Treaty of Ghent, ending the War of 1812 between the

United States and England, was signed December 24, 1814, yet ten days later General Andrew Jackson fought and won the historic Battle of New Orleans, because news of the peace treaty had not reached the United States. If there had been a means of fast overseas communication this battle would not have taken place—and Jackson might not later have become President of the United States.

Canals, steamboats and new roads facilitated communication, but news and messages were still unable to travel faster than slow vessels and horses. The coming of railroads in the 1830s speeded up the transmission of letters and printed material, but only between the relatively few places connected by tracks.

New discoveries about electricity aroused the interest of Joseph Henry, a philosophy professor at the Albany (New York) Academy, who had read about the experiments of the European scientists. In 1831 Professor Henry suspended nearly one mile of wire along the walls and ceiling of a classroom, connecting one end to a battery and the other to a U-shaped piece of iron. A magnetized iron bar was placed atop a metal rod at the mouth of the "U" and so arranged that the bar could pivot in any direction, like a weathervane. Near one end of the bar was a small bell.

When Henry sent a charge of electricity through the wire to the iron "U" the current magnetized the metal, the magnetism attracted the pivoted bar and made it swing around and strike the bell. By this experiment Henry established that it was possible to shoot electricity through a very long wire and make it activate a signal at a distance.

It was this discovery that enabled a portrait painter named Samuel Finley Breese Morse to perfect a method of swift communication—the telegraph.

Born on April 27, 1791, in Charlestown, Massachusetts, Sam Morse eventually graduated from Yale University, became interested in art and went to England to study painting under the direction of Benjamin West. In England his work with paints and brushes shared time with his reading about the electrical experiments performed by Michael Faraday, Volta and others; and Morse developed such an urge to explore this new science that his painting became of secondary importance.

On the basis of Faraday's and Henry's experiments, Morse was convinced that he could make a signaling device to transmit messages over long distances by wire. In 1835 in New York City he built his first crude telegraph. He attached a pencil to a magnet above a roll of white paper which was unwound slowly by a clock spring. The closing of an electric circuit at one end of the wire sent current to the magnet and brought the attached pencil into contact with the moving paper. If the current was cut off quickly, the pencil made a dot on the paper. If the charge remained for a longer interval, the pencil stayed against the moving paper and the mark was a dash. Morse then devised a system of dots and dashes to represent letters of the alphabet, and by means of this "Morse Code" he was able to send words electrically as far as a wire could reach.

After making improved models and giving various demonstrations, Morse was granted thirty thousand dollars by the government to build a telegraph line from Washington, D. C., to Baltimore, Maryland. The line was completed in May, 1844, and on that day the first message was sent from Washington to Baltimore. It was a four-word sentence composed by Miss Annie Ellsworth, daughter of the Commissioner of Patents and a good friend of Morse's. The message read: "What hath God wrought."

The government proposed to use the telegraph as part of the Post Office Department, but in 1845 came the threat of war with Mexico, and the government lost interest in Morse's invention. Morse and some of his associates then organized the Magnetic Telegraph Company, the first of several private stock companies operating telegraph lines in various parts of the nation. (Later these smaller companies were combined to form The Western Union Telegraph Company.)

After the United States clashed with Mexico over boundary disputes in 1846, newspapers found that the "lightning wire" could flash news of the fighting in minutes, and a group of New York publishers joined forces to pool telegraphic reports from their war correspondents at the front. They called their new organization The Associated Press.

The telegraph more than proved its worth, and when the Mexican War ended, more and more railroad companies began to use telegraphy to control rail traffic. As telegraph lines unrolled westward, cattle ranchers could communicate with shipping companies in the East to arrange for the transfer of cattle from freight trains to ships for transportation across the ocean. Manufacturers could place orders for raw materials more swiftly than ever before. Farmers could negotiate quickly for the sale and shipment of grain and perishable crops. Settlers once starved for news were kept informed of goings-on in Washington and other cities. Isolation of communities was slowly disappearing, and a widely scattered population was being drawn closer together to make a strong and growing union, thanks to a spark of electricity and Sam Morse's singing wires.

Less dramatic than the telegraph, yet destined to help stitch together the strong industrial fabric of the nation, was another great invention—the sewing machine.

Devices called "sewing machines" were invented in Europe as long ago as 1755, when a British patent for such a device was issued to Charles F. Weisenthal. Actually it was not a machine at all. It was simply a two-pointed needle with an eye in the center, designed to be used by hand and passed back and forth through cloth without having to turn the needle around.

In 1790 another British patent was issued to Thomas Saint for a simple machine that produced a chain stitch, and in 1804 John Duncan invented an improved device that incorporated some of the basic principles of the sewing machine as we know it today.

In 1830 many European countries were building up their armed forces, creating a need for uniforms. Tailors who made clothing by hand could not meet the heavy demand, but there was no alternative until 1830, when Bartholomey Thimonier, a French tailor, patented a wooden sewing machine which gave promise of being practical and efficient. Thimonier kept devising improvements for his machine and finally convinced the French government that his invention could produce clothing much faster than any hand-tailoring. The government bought eighty of his machines and began to turn out thousands of military uniforms.

Scores of tailors were thrown out of work because of this new labor-saving device, and the same kind of resentment and anger that had plagued John Kay, James Hargreaves and others in years past now welled up in the tailors. Impelled by mob talk and mob spirit they descended upon Thimonier's shop, chopped his sewing machines to splinters, then set the place on fire. They then delivered an ultimatum to Thimonier.

"Get out of Paris and stay out!" they told him. "You and

your machines have taken the bread out of our mouths. If you try to build more we'll come back and kill you!"

The frightened Thimonier left Paris, but was determined to build more sewing machines. He did make a few more which he sold for ten dollars each, and once again his shop was raided by a mob that threatened his life. By 1848 he had made more improvements in his invention and managed to start another clothing factory, but the "February Revolution" of the industrial workers which brought about the abdication of King Louis Philippe also resulted in the wanton destruction of Thimonier's shop, and he finally admitted defeat.

In 1832, while Thimonier was at work in France, an American inventor, Walter Hunt of New York City, created a machine which would "sew, stitch and seam cloth." After a few years of struggle to improve and perfect the device he suggested that his daughter, Caroline, set herself up in the business of making corsets, using his creation. In talking about this proposal Caroline said that such an establishment would be likely to deprive many seamstresses of jobs, a possibility she preferred to avoid. Her father finally agreed with her, and to benefit society he deliberately failed to patent his invention and undoubtedly lost a fortune.

Hunt did, however, invent other devices which were successful. One of these was created within three hours so that Hunt could repay a loan of fifteen dollars which he had borrowed from a friend named J. R. Chapin. One afternoon Hunt bent a length of ordinary wire into an unusual shape, sharpened one end of it to a point, and obtained a patent for a "Dress-Pin," then sold his rights to Chapin for four hundred dollars. The invention made millions for its manufacturers and is still in wide use. We call it the "safety pin."

Other inventors with less of a conscience than Hunt's applied for patents on various kinds of sewing machines, but none was successful until a New England farm youth named Elias Howe, Jr., applied his talents to the problem.

In the growing United States, as in Europe, the demand for ready-made clothing was increasing. The government wanted more uniforms for its armed forces. Hundreds of New England whalers and other seamen, returning home after months or years at sea, promptly bought "shore duds," and the tailors who made all clothing by hand were unable to keep pace with orders.

Elias Howe, Jr., was born in 1819 on a rock-strewn farm near Spencer, Massachusetts, where he spent part of his boyhood "bound out" to a neighboring farmer as a chore boy, milking cows, pitching hay and doing other farm work. Despite objections from his parents he quit his job and went to Lowell to work in a factory which produced cotton-spinning machinery, but when the panic of 1837 hit the country Howe and scores of others lost their factory jobs.

The eighteen-year-old Howe went to Boston, where he tramped from shop to shop seeking work. In a small, dirty, cluttered machine shop Howe met the owner, Ari Davis, an eccentric genius who today would probably be labeled a "screwball" by some people. Davis was frequently asked for help and advice by professors from Harvard University, for whom he also made laboratory apparatus; and while he often received customers in friendly fashion, he also was known to shout at them angrily at the top of his lungs and even to order them out of his shop. He wore ill-fitting bright red, green or other gaily colored clothes which attracted attention wherever he went. Davis was evidently impressed by Elias Howe's personality and knowledge, for he hired him on the spot.

Two years later, in 1839, Howe's future was shaped by

two men who called on Davis. One was a mechanic who had tried to invent a knitting machine. The other was a wealthy promoter who was interested in financing the invention. There was only one trouble with the knitting machine—it wouldn't work!—and the men wanted Davis to tell them what was wrong. Davis' workmen, including young Howe, gathered around to look at the contraption.

After inspecting the machine Davis dropped it on a workbench and waved his arms in a gesture of futility. Shouting so that he could even be heard on the street he cried, "Why the devil are you wasting your time on a knitting machine?"

"Wasting time?" the capitalist said. "But we—"

"Yes, wasting time!" Davis interrupted. "This is no good. You won't ever make it work." He shook a pointing finger in the customer's face. "If you want to do something worthwhile, something profitable, go out and make a sewing machine!"

"Hah! I wish I could—but you know as well as I do that it can't be done."

"Oh, bosh!" Davis shouted. "I could make one myself, anytime."

"You could, huh? All right, Davis, you make a sewing machine and I'll make you a fortune."

The talk returned to the knitting machine and there is no indication that Davis or his wealthy customer ever again discussed the invention of a good sewing machine. Elias Howe, who had overheard the conversation, was deeply impressed by the fine clothes and distinguished appearance of the wealthy gentleman, and especially by his promise that a sewing machine could bring a fortune to its inventor.

Howe, who was then twenty years old, did not take any immediate action, although he gave continued thought to the possibility. Two years later the thought turned to reality, and by 1844 he devoted all of his time to the invention of a sewing machine. In May, 1845, he completed his first working model and tested it by sewing all the seams in two suits of clothes, one for himself and one for George Fisher, a friend in whose home he worked.

He obtained a patent, one-half of which he assigned to Fisher for five hundred dollars, the other half going to Howe's father for two thousand dollars. As a result Howe no longer owned his patent and had no way to produce the machine. His brother Amasa suggested that it might be patented in England in Howe's name, in which case the machines could be produced and sold there.

Amasa took a machine to England and sold it to William Thomas of Cheapside, who was to obtain a patent in his own name and pay royalties to Elias Howe for each machine sold. Thomas also agreed to hire Elias to work on improvements for the machine in his shop.

Howe, his wife and three children went to England, but in the weeks that followed he quarreled with Thomas and was fired. Howe had nothing and the English patent was owned by Thomas. With money borrowed from friends Howe bought passage to the United States for his wife and children, and in 1849 he returned himself, just in time to see his sick wife before she died.

He discovered that several of his sewing machines were being manufactured by people who had infringed the American patents, and with the help of his father and George Fisher, Howe fought them in the courts and won. With the money awarded him he bought back his interests in the original patent and became its sole owner.

With the advent of Howe's machine a new and vital clothing industry began to build; and several other inventors created improvements in Howe's original and gave added thrust to the Industrial Revolution. William O. Grover, James E. Gibbs and others contributed more new ideas. David M. Smyth invented the first machine for sewing leather soles on shoes and also made the first machine for the sewing of pages in bookbinding.

Allen C. Wilson, of Pittsfield, Massachusetts, and his partner, Nathaniel Wheeler, invented the "rotary hook" which distinguished the famous Wheeler & Wilson machine. These two men also produced one of the most ingenious combinations in the sewing machine line. One account describes it this way:

The apparatus had the appearance, externally, of a small parlor sideboard or other similar piece of furniture. On lifting the front there was seen a handsome set of piano keys. On closing it and turning back a hoop on the top, there opened to the view a complete sewing machine, conveniently arranged. Concealed below, within side doors, were two pedals, one for the music, the other for the sewing machine. Thus, by the use of one of these ingenious contrivances, when the lady operating the machine became tired of playing at sewing, she could change her foot to the other pedal, open the melodeon part and discourse music!

Probably the man who deserves most of the credit for "putting a sewing machine in every home" and for making it a mighty factor in the Industrial Revolution was Isaac Merritt Singer, a cabinetmaker, mechanic, one-time actor and theater manager from Oswego, New York.

An inventor of sorts, Singer went to Boston in 1850 with a working model of a wood-carving machine which he invented. In Boston a man named George Zieber paid Singer three thousand dollars for the rights to make and sell the machine in

Massachusetts. Zieber also arranged for Singer to build machines in a shop owned by Orson C. Phelps, who made and repaired various kinds of sewing machines, many of which were on hand waiting to be fixed. Singer inspected them with much curiosity.

"Have you seen any of these before?" Phelps asked.

"No, I haven't," Singer answered.

"It's a wonderful invention, all right, but we repair more than we sell because they're always breaking down in one way or another. If a few things could be corrected, and if an improved machine could be made to sell for forty dollars or less, it would make a fortune for the inventor." He showed Singer a few features that he believed needed improvement.

Phelps' words kept echoing in Singer's mind—*make a fortune, make a fortune, forty dollars, make a fortune.* The next night he sat up late and made three sketches showing how the machines on exhibition could be made substantially better. In the morning he discussed the drawings with Phelps and Zieber.

"They seem practicable," Phelps said. "The question is whether or not your improvements will work. You'll have to make a model and find out."

"But I have no money to buy materials, and no place to work."

"How much money would you need?" Zieber wanted to know.

Singer shrugged. "Thirty or forty dollars, at least."

"I'll lend you forty dollars," Zieber said.

"And I'll help you do the mechanical work here in my shop," Phelps added.

They shook hands and Singer said, "If we succeed, we'll all share equally in whatever may come of the work."

The job was not easy, as Singer himself later related. "I worked day and night," he said, "sleeping but three or four hours out of the twenty-four and eating generally but once a day, as I knew I must get a machine made for forty dollars or not get it at all. The machine was completed the night of the eleventh day from the day it was commenced. About nine o'clock that evening we got the parts of the machine together and commenced trying it."

"The first attempt to sew was unsuccessful," he went on, "and the workmen, who were tired out with almost unremitting work, left me one by one, intimating that it was a failure. I continued trying the machine with Zieber, who furnished the forty dollars, to hold the lamp for me, but in a nervous condition to which I had been reduced by incessant work and anxiety, was unsuccessful in getting the machine to sew tight stitches.

"About midnight I started with Zieber to the hotel where I boarded. Upon the way we sat down on a pile of boards and Zieber asked me if I had not noticed that the loose loops of thread on the upper side of the cloth came from the needle. It then flashed upon me that I had forgotten to adjust the tension upon the needle thread. Zieber and I went back to the shop. I adjusted the tension, tried the machine and sewed five stitches perfectly, when the thread broke. The perfection of those stitches satisfied me that the machine was a success, and I stopped work, went to the hotel and had a sound sleep. By three o'clock the next day I had the machine finished and started with it to New York, where I employed Mr. Charles M. Keller to get out a patent for it."

The patent was issued to Singer in 1851, and he immediately proceeded to build a factory and opened beautifully decorated and carpeted salesrooms where attractive women, trained as operators, demonstrated Singer's machines for potential buyers.

In the meantime Elias Howe launched a legal attack against Singer, charging that Singer had infringed a Howe patent. There were substantial differences between some parts of the Singer and Howe machines. Howe's was operated by a hand crank which had to be turned by the user, whereas Singer's was run by a foot treadle so that the operator had both hands free. In the Howe machine the needle moved back and forth horizontally; in the Singer it moved up and down vertically. However, the needle invented by Howe had its eye at the point, and Singer had used the same kind of needle. This was the basis for the court battle, which in 1854 when Singer was ordered to pay Howe $28,000, plus $10 for every machine sold thereafter.

Ironically, the eye-pointed needle had also been invented by Walter Hunt, the man who failed to patent his sewing machine in 1832 because he didn't want to put seamstresses out of work. Hunt tried to get a patent in 1854, but it was refused on the grounds that he had abandoned his invention years earlier.

Subsequently Singer and Howe agreed to pool their sewing machine patents to license several companies to mass-produce the machines, with royalty payments being made to the inventors. When Elias Howe died in 1867 at the age of forty-eight, he had received more than two million dollars in royalties. Isaac Singer spent more than $25,000 a week to advertise sewing machines. He built more factories and lavish sales offices, and within twelve years he was selling a thousand machines a week at a profit of a thousand dollars a day.

Many other inventors added new attachments or improvements to the basic sewing machine—attachments for hemming, ruffling, sewing buttonholes, edging, or for sewing harness, shoes, hats, carpets, rubber goods, tents, flags and other products. In Massachusetts alone the boot-and-shoe industry, after being equipped with sewing machines, saved nearly eight million dollars in labor costs in one year. A Connecticut shirt manufacturer, whose factory produced nearly ten thousand shirts a week, said that he used four hundred sewing machines, any one of which would do the work previously done by five people sewing by hand.

The sewing machine revolutionized the clothing business, shoemaking, sailmaking, bookbinding and scores of other crafts. It rapidly increased the demand for raw cotton, flax and wool, for finished cloth, leather, rubber and all sorts of other goods used in manufactured products that required sewing. Equally important, it became a treasured possession of American women and an invaluable addition to millions of homes not only in the United States but also throughout the world.

Although the sewing machine today is streamlined and electrified, its principles are basically the same as those devised by Hunt, Howe, Singer and their contemporaries more than 125 years ago, and it continues to be one of the greatest industrial and domestic inventions of all time.

CHAPTER 8

Black Stones, Flowing Gold and Cooked Iron

In 1812 Colonel Shoemaker of Pottsville, Pennsylvania, took nine wagonloads of anthracite (hard) coal to Philadelphia to sell, but most of the prospective customers he visited told him the same thing: "Get that stuff out of here. We've tried it before and it won't burn. It's no good and we don't want any."

It was true that nine years earlier, in 1803, the first mining company, the Lehigh Coal Mine Company, had been founded and had shipped anthracite coal from its mines in Lehigh to the city fathers of Philadelphia, who proposed to use it to power city-owned machinery. The coal could not be made to burn, so it was broken into small pieces and used like gravel to cover sidewalks. "These are only black stones," the city authorities declared. "They'll never burn."

But the black stones had been burning in the mountains of Pennsylvania for a long time, mostly in the forges of blacksmiths. Colonel Shoemaker finally gave quantities of his coal to several Philadelphia business firms "on trial," asking that they experiment with it. At one of these companies, the Fairmount Nail and Wire Works, workmen spent an entire morning trying to burn the black stones in a furnace. They lit paper and wood shavings and small sticks, and when these were blazing they stirred them around and around in the coal. By lunch time the coal had not caught fire, and the workmen went to eat, leaving the kindling to smolder and smoke.

When they came back they were amazed to discover that the furnace door was white-hot and that the black stones were glowing brightly. Thus by accident they learned that the secret was to put lighted kindling under the coal and let the coal alone instead of stirring it as they had done in the past.

The word spread quickly and other companies flooded the mineowners with orders. New mining companies began to dig coal from the hills, and in 1820 the Pennsylvania mines shipped 365 tons. Within ten years this figure totaled almost 360,000 tons, and in 1873 the mines produced more than 22 million tons and employed some 50,000 miners and laborers. Coal mining had become a major industry.

Coal was more efficient than wood for heating. By a slow-heat process, or cooking, coal also produced coal gas, which came into use in the 1820s for lighting many homes and city streets. Thousands of people, however, could not afford it and continued to use tallow candles or lamps that burned foul-smelling whale oil. Then in 1846 coal yielded another secret when Dr. Abraham Gesner, a Canadian geologist, succeeded in extracting from it a distilled liquid which he called *kerosene* (from the Greek *keros* meaning "wax").

This "coal oil" could be burned in lamps and did not stink as whale oil did. One by one new companies were organized to manufacture and sell coal oil, and by the late 1850s more than thirty of these plants were in operation in the United States.

Oddly enough, all during the years when men were experimenting to obtain oil from coal, and after they had succeeded and were selling coal oil in big quantities, another kind of oil was oozing out of the ground in Pennsylvania and other places and was long looked upon as a nuisance, except to the American Indian.

Long before the white man invaded their lands the Seneca Indians in western New York State skimmed black oil from the waters of the Seneca Lake and used it to mix with their war paints, to massage their bodies, to heal wounds, and in their sacred ceremonies. The thick liquid became known as "Seneca oil," or sometimes as "rock oil" or "fossil oil," but its real value was not recognized for a long time. In Pennsylvania and western Virginia there were men who made their livelihood by sinking "salt wells," pumping out brine (salt water) from which they obtained salt crystals. Frequently the brine came up along with quantities of crude oil which the salt sellers looked upon with disgust.

In 1849, Samuel Kier, a Pennsylvanian, collected a few barrels of oil from salt wells owned by his father, a druggist, near Tarentum, Pennsylvania. Kier poured the oil into a number of half-pint bottles labeled "Genuine Petroleum. None Genuine without the signature, S. M. Kier." If oil massages had been helpful to the Indians, why not sell the stuff to the white man as a medicinal ointment?

Kier at first marketed his oil through drugstores and became so successful that he later traveled through many states in a golden chariot from which he made his sales pitch to crowds on street corners. He reaped a rich harvest from his oil concoction at fifty cents a bottle.

One day while Kier was making his spiel in Cleveland, Ohio, a young boy walked down the street along the fringe of the crowd. There is no evidence that the boy listened to Kier or even gave him more than a passing glance, but fate was to plunge this youngster into an oil business that would make him one of the world's wealthiest men.

The boy's name was John Davison Rockefeller.

In 1854, while John D. Rockefeller was a high school student in Cleveland, a New York attorney, George H. Bissell, learned from a Dartmouth College professor that crude oil found floating on streams in Pennsylvania could be refined to produce kerosene. Bissell went to the village of Titusville, Pennsylvania and saw the film of oil floating on Oil Creek. Local inhabitants who wanted to get some of the oil simply spread blankets on the water, then wrung out the sticky fluid which the blankets had absorbed.

Bissell quietly bought more than a hundred acres of land along Oil Creek, then returned to New York and with his law partner, J. G. Eveleth, founded the Pennsylvania Rock Oil Company.

Others were also discovering the possibilities in oil. Samuel Kier hired a chemist to teach him how to distill crude oil and obtain what Kier called "carbon oil." Carbon oil could not be used in kerosene lamps, so Kier invented a special kind of lamp to burn his new-found product.

With an increasing demand for crude oil, those in the business searched anxiously for some way to obtain oil in larger quantities. One day George Bissell saw one of Samuel Kier's handbills, part of which carried a picture of a derrick, or tower, representing the salt well from which Kier obtained his crude oil. Here, perhaps, was the answer. People drilled wells for brine—why not for oil?

Bissell discussed his idea with several friends in New Haven, Connecticut, who saw an opportunity to make money. They organized the Seneca Oil Company and hired a retired railroad conductor, Edwin L. Drake, to go to Titusville and experiment in drilling for oil.

After a preliminary visit in 1857 Drake and his family went to live in Titusville, where he built a wooden derrick and began to drill. After months of discouraging work Drake's perseverance paid off when, on August 21, 1859, crude oil flowed to the surface, bubbled out of a pipe in his well and spilled onto the ground. This first drilled oil well was a success, marking the beginning of an industry that was to become one of the greatest and most important in the history of the world.

News of Drake's strike flowed like oil itself, and the oil rush of '59 raised echoes of the gold rush of '49. "Wildcatters" invaded Pennsylvania to drill here, there, everywhere, gambling on possible gushers. Unscrupulous men printed phony oil stock certificates and swindled hundreds of gullible investors. In Cleveland, Ohio, a group of businessmen wanted to invest in the flowing gold, but wisely decided to learn more about it. They sent John D. Rockefeller to Titusville to get the facts.

Rockefeller was then only twenty years old, working as a produce and commission merchant in Cleveland, in partnership with M. A. Clark. He had little or no interest in the oil business, but he was widely known to be honest, thrifty, level-headed and shrewd.

Young Rockefeller went to Titusville, saw the wells and asked endless questions of scores of people. Analyzing the answers, he returned to Cleveland and told his friends, in effect, "My advice is to wait a while and see whether or not there is a continuing demand for oil. If there is, then I recommend that you go into the refining business and not into production."

In other words, let someone else drill the wells and supply the crude oil to be refined into kerosene.

Each new petroleum well struck a blow to another great American industry which was at its peak in the 1850s—whaling. For years Yankee whaleships and Yankee sailors had roamed the seas killing whales and bringing home cargoes of whale oil and whalebone. Whale oil was used in lamps to provide light in homes and on streets, but it cost two dollars a gallon or more and had an obnoxious odor. When oil-refining methods yielded kerosene the whaling industry was doomed. One of the world's greatest whaling centers, New Bedford, Massachusetts, became a graveyard for whaleships and a drydock for the men who sailed them.

When the Civil War began in 1861 most of the oil wells shut down. In 1862 Samuel Andrews, who operated a small refinery in Cleveland, asked Rockefeller and Clark for a cash loan to expand his business. By that time Rockefeller was convinced that there would be a growing demand for oil, so he loaned Andrews several thousand dollars and set up a new partnership of Andrews & Clark.

When the war ended in 1865 there was a great clamor for kerosene, and John Rockefeller decided that profits from oil would be much greater than those from groceries. At the age of twenty-five he bought Clark's share of the company for $75,000 and went into partnership with Andrews.

To expand the company's operations Rockefeller needed more money. He approached Henry M. Flagler, from whom Rockefeller and Clark had bought grain, and who was now trying to finance a "perfect horseshoe" he had invented. Young Rockefeller did not expect Flagler himself to come up with a loan, but he knew that Flagler had married the niece of Stephen V. Harkness, a wealthy distiller, and Rockefeller proposed to reach Harkness through Flagler.

With this in mind he invited Flagler to become a partner in the oil business, and with Flagler's help he induced Harkness to invest $70,000 in the firm as a "silent partner."

By 1870 kerosene was being produced in such quantities that its price began to go down, and at the same time the railroads were raising prices for shipping it. As a result many small refiners in the Cleveland area were fearful that they could not stay in business. John Rockefeller and his partners, sensing the opportunity for more expansion, bought some twenty refineries and organized a new company with one million dollars' worth of stock at one hundred dollars a share. The new company was named after the Standard Works, one of their refineries, and became famous as the Standard Oil Company of Ohio. Its principal product was kerosene, still in wide demand for lighting.

Lighting, however, was in a state of change. In some homes and towns kerosene had given way to gas. Although coal gas was still in use, it had been found that a natural gas could be obtained from the oil wells, and both types were far more efficient than kerosene. Then in 1879 a new invention threatened to supplant both gas and kerosene for illumination. In that year Thomas A. Edison made public demonstrations of his amazing electric light bulb.

Tom Edison, who had only three months of formal schooling, had spent much of his boyhood tinkering with machines and electricity, worked as a newsboy on the Grand Trunk Railroad in Michigan, and as a youth became an expert telegraph operator.

Restless and longing to do original research, he went to Boston in 1868 and got a job with Western Union, but about a year later he quit and traveled to New York, hoping for more challenging work.

While he was seeking employment the financial world was panicked by a frenzy of price changes for stocks and bonds. Prices went up and down so swiftly that the electric stock tickers were unable to keep abreast of them. In an office where Edison went to apply for work the ticker stopped completely. Stockbrokers and customers were frantic.

"It's busted! The ticker's busted!" someone shouted.

"Hey! Somebody get this thing going!" another yelled.

The manager and his assistants fiddled with the mechanism but were unable to get it started.

"I can fix it," Edison said.

The manager stared at the young stranger for a moment. "Well, fix it, then!" he said. "Go on, go on, get it going!"

It took Edison about two hours to repair the ticker, but then it worked perfectly. In gratitude the company hired him immediately.

Later in 1869 Edison invented and patented a new kind of stock ticker, much speedier than those then in use. A New York stock organization asked him to name a price for his patent. Edison later revealed that he intended to ask for five thousand dollars, but it seemed such a large sum that he was afraid to mention it. Instead he said, "What do you think it's worth?"

"We'll give you forty thousand dollars—not a penny more," the company officials said.

Edison was dumbfounded, but managed to stammer his thanks. He used the money to hire a number of workmen and set up a shop in Newark, New Jersey, to manufacture stock tickers. Later he gave up this specialized work, deciding to explore a variety of fields for new inventions, and in 1876

An artist's concept of craftsmen at work in pre-industrial Boston.

Sometimes industry came first and communities grew around it.

UNION IRON COMPANY.

A. PARDEE, Prest. G.R. WILSON, Vice Prest.
GEO. BEALS Treas. T. GUILFORD SMITH, Secy
JAMES JENKINS, Supt

BUFFALO, N.Y.

PIG IRON, BARS, SHAFTING & RAILS.
BEAMS, CHANNELS & PLATES,
IRON BRIDGES & IRON SHIPS.

WM. H. WALLACE & CO., Agents, 131 Washington St., New York City.

Richard Trevithick's steam locomotive.

On Christmas Day in 1830, scheduled steam railroad service began in America.

The Rocket built by George Stephenson continues to be recognized as the ancestor to the modern steam locomotive.

Union Pacific Railroad's new 8500 horsepower gas-turbine locomotive showing two units and fuel tank.

Robert Fulton's *Clermont*

The iron steamship *Great Eastern* which succeeded in laying the first transatlantic undersea cable.

irst of the "horseless carriages"—the Duryea.

Henry Ford driving his original car,
the Quadricycle.

First big step toward mass production came with the moving
auto chassis assembly line at the Ford Motor Co.

This was the only known method of cotton picking—hand power.

Now one man and a mechanical cotton picker can do work that once required scores of field hands.

Isaac Singer's original sewing machine.

Cyrus McCormick's original reaping machine.

Textile weaver at work on a large hand-operated loom.

Samuel Slater, "Father of American Manufacturers."

Elias Howe, inventor of the sewing machine.

James Watt, whose steam engine put the Industrial Revolution into high gear.

Cyrus Hale McCormick, inventor of the reaping machine.

Eli Whitney, whose cotton gin revolutionized southern agriculture.

Joseph Henry, pioneer in telegraphy.

Thomas Alva Edison, whose electric light bulb revolutionized lighting and created new industries

Alexander Graham Bell at the opening of the New York-Chicago line, 1892.

Wilhelm Konrad von Roentgen, discoverer of X-rays.

Guglielmo Marconi, inventor of wireless.

Lee De Forest and his "Audion" tube.

Enrico Fermi, leader of pioneer science team who built the world's first nuclear reactor.

Charles Goodyear's discovery of the vulcanization of rubber was a happy accident.

Edwin L. Drake (in "stovepipe") discusses operation of America's first oil well in Titusville, Pennsylvania.

Alexander Graham Bell lecturing in Salem, Massachusetts. A telephone is placed before his audience while he communicates with his laboratory in Boston, fourteen miles away.

An early model of a typewriter produced by E. Remington & Sons, based on the original model submitted by Latham Sholes and James Densmore.

Dr. Robert Goddard with a pioneer rocket. He opened the way to space exploration.

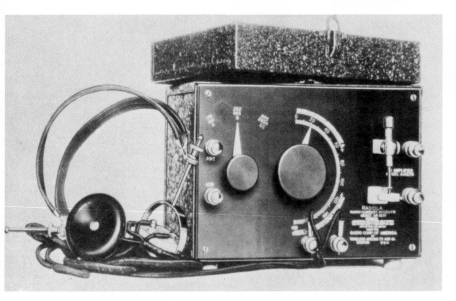

Early model of an RCA crystal set radio.

This was radio in the 1920's.

Scale model of world's first atomic pile for controlled release of nuclear energy built by Dr. Enrico Fermi and associates.

Scale model of first nuclear reactor built in racquets court under Stagg Field, Chicago.

The submarine *USS Nautilus* brought atomic power to New York Harbor for the first time, January 17, 1955.

N.S. Savannah, world's first nuclear cargo-passenger ship, under way on power furnished from her atomic reactor.

RCA Computer.

Bell System's Telstar experimental
communications satellite.

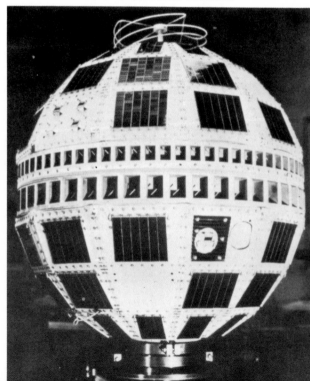

he moved his shop to Menlo Park, New Jersey. It was there in 1878 that he conceived and developed the electric light bulb.

An electric light, as such, was not entirely new. A crude arc lamp was made by Sir Humphry Davy, the British scientist, in the early 1800s, and improved arc lamps were used in 1860 as street lights in New York and other cities. They were big, glaring and expensive, and their light brightened and dimmed erratically, so that they were not at all suited to home use. Modern homes in the 1870s were lighted by kerosene or gas, and Edison set out to make an electric light that could compete with these fuels.

Briefly, he sought to burn a carbon filament, or thread, in a small glass globe. He actually ran tests on several thousand different fibers before he finally decided on carbonized cotton thread. By installing the carbonized fiber in the globe or bulb, and then creating a vacuum by pumping out the air, he was able to make the filament white hot by shooting an electric current through it, and it burned for many hours without failure.

When news of his invention spread, the prices of stock in gas companies and oil refineries tumbled because people thought there would soon be little demand for gas or kerosene.

John Rockefeller and his associates did not share this belief, and gradually they bought out other refineries and built an oil empire which, in 1882, became known as the Standard Oil Trust. Under a complex agreement the trust held the securities of forty-one investors in forty different companies, including the Standard Oil Company of New Jersey.

Many people who could not yet afford electricity continued to buy kerosene, and the Standard Oil Trust found profitable markets for oil in Europe, South America, Africa and the Orient. Gradually new companies sprang up in foreign lands

in competition with Standard Oil—companies that grew into
Royal Dutch Shell, British Petroleum and the French Petroleum Company.

As markets and prices for kerosene went down, another
invention promised to put new life into the oil industry. In
1893 the "horseless carriage" was born and needed gasoline
for its engine. The automobile age was destined to revolutionize transportation, provide thousands of jobs and create
a tremendous demand for gasoline, oil and oil by-products.

Oil companies competing with Standard Oil branded the
trust as a monopoly and brought suits in court to break it up.
Legal battles were waged for several years, and in 1911 under
a decision of the Supreme Court of the United States the
Standard Oil Trust was separated into thirty-four unrelated
companies. In that year these companies, for the first time, sold
more gasoline than kerosene in the United States.

New companies came into existence to compete in the
growing market—organizations such as The Texas Company
(Texaco) and the Gulf Oil Corporation. Today the research
programs of the oil industry have brought us a long way from
Samuel Kier's bottled Indian ointment. They have given us
aviation fuel, diesel fuel, naphtha, medicinal oils and creams,
cosmetics, rust preventives, wood preservatives, grease for
various purposes, asphalt shingles and roof and road coatings,
synthetic rubber, anesthetics, antifreeze, plastics, insecticides,
waxes and polishes, chewing gum and food coatings. Oil wells
throughout the world produce more than eight billion barrels
of the flowing gold in a gigantic industry that began with the
little bubbling well of Edwin L. Drake in Titusville, Pennsylvania, more than a hundred years ago.

In 1859, the year in which Drake drilled America's first oil
well, another man was beginning a career in a different kind

of industry that was to grow into a major economic segment of the United States. His name was Andrew Carnegie, and he was to become to the iron and steel industry what John D. Rockefeller was to the oil business.

Iron has been used by man for at least six thousand years. Long before the Christian era, men fashioned iron implements from meteorites, which they called "metal from heaven." In ancient times iron was considered to be as valuable as gold is today and was made into beads, bracelets and rings by the early Egyptians and Romans, who also used it to make spears, daggers and tools. Since meteoric iron was scarce, it is evident that the ancients discovered, perhaps by accident, how to produce the metal by burning the oxygen out of iron ore. By medieval times, iron was being used to make suits of armor, chariots, swords and other useful articles.

Records dating as far back as four hundred years before Christ show that the people of India learned to transform iron into steel, as did the Persians, the Chinese, the Greeks and the Romans.

The first ironworks in America was built about 1620 along Falling Creek, Virginia. The iron ore itself was scraped from rocks or dug from swamps and was called "bog ore," a name which was still used by the settlers in Massachusetts and Connecticut many years later. In addition, the New England hills were found to contain heavy iron ore deposits, and eventually a number of miners dug them out to supply forges and blast furnaces in a growing iron industry. Some of the wrought-iron candlesticks, weathervanes and other early pieces found in some of our antique shops today were made from the New England ore.

Not all of the pioneer craftsmen engaged in honest work. Some who were skilled in metalworking were experts in skulduggery, such as counterfeiting of coins. Perhaps one reason for this was that the British government (before the American Revolution) made it unlawful for inhabitants of the American colonies to build any mill for rolling iron or for making steel. The colonies were, however, encouraged to export "pig iron" to England, where it would be fashioned into finished goods to be exported for sale to colonists.

"Pig iron" was so called because it apparently reminded someone of baby pigs at nursing time! The molten metal was poured into a straight mold having other molds at right angles to it, like a capital E with added horizontal strokes. The long mold was called the "sow" and the shorter pieces were the "pigs." When the bars were later cooled and separated, the "sow" was also cut into "pigs."

The British prohibition against American rolling mills was inspired by the fear of British manufacturers that they would be forced out of business if the colonists were permitted to manufacture goods from their own raw materials.

As the demand for iron tools, nails, weapons and utensils increased, more and more furnaces were built to smelt ore. Early smelting was done by burning charcoal, and to obtain enough charcoal to produce about two tons of iron, men had to cut down about one acre of trees every day. In the eighteenth century Pennsylvania produced quantities of iron, and many people established "iron plantations" covering thousands of acres of forested land—similar to the South's cotton plantations, except that the "crop" was metallic.

In 1844 a team of surveyors working in northern Michigan accidentally discovered a huge deposit of iron ore. In the years that followed, this area, along with Minnesota and Wisconsin, became (and still is) the world's largest commercial iron-mining region.

It was not until about 1725 that the first *steel* was produced in America by Samuel Higley of Simsbury, Connecticut, and some nine years later a steelworks was founded in Trenton, New Jersey.

At first steel was made by "cooking" iron bars in charcoal for long periods of time. The iron absorbed carbon from the charcoal and the resulting combination was steel. The "steel age," however, had its small beginnings in 1847 when William Kelly, owner of an ironworks in Eddyville, Kentucky, was in great need of wood for making charcoal. To supply this need he would have to pay high prices for hauling wood from timberlands about seven miles from his plant, and he sought some other solution to his heating problem.

Quite by accident Kelly noticed one day that a batch of molten iron seemed to be made even hotter when it was struck by a blast of cold air. Experiments convinced him that the oxygen in the cold air destroyed impurities in the iron, but when he described his theory to his wife and her father they had him examined by a doctor because they thought he was crazy! The doctor, however, having some knowledge of chemistry and physics, declared that Kelly was both sane and smart.

Kelly eventually built a special furnace through which cold air could be blown into molten pig iron, making it capable of being hammered into various shapes without breaking.

About seven years after Kelly made his discovery Henry Bessemer, an English metallurgist, knowing nothing of Kelly's findings, invented a similar process of refining iron. Then Robert Mushet, a Scot, found that he could make steel by adding small amounts of carbon and manganese to the iron after it had been blasted with the cold air. This was the basis of what is now known as the Bessemer process, although it was the original brainchild of William Kelly and Robert Mushet.

Since iron ore was plentiful in Pennsylvania, it was logical that a growing iron industry took shape in Pittsburgh, which was already a thriving boomtown in 1848 when Andrew Carnegie came to America from Scotland as a thirteen-year-old boy. Soon he went to work for the Pennsylvania Railroad, became a telegraph operator, and by the time he was twenty-four he was superintendent of the road's western Division. The Pennsylvania and other railroads were clamoring for iron and steel for new rails, locomotives, wheels, cars and other equipment, and young Carnegie soon realized that fortunes could be made in the iron and steel industry. Accordingly, he used his savings to buy part ownership of two companies—one that made steel axles for railroad cars, and one that built iron bridges.

The companies did a thriving business, and Carnegie invested some of his profits in another firm that manufactured railroad sleeping cars. This investment was also successful and enabled him to buy stock in an oil company and other growing businesses. By 1863, when he was twenty-eight years old, Carnegie earned a salary of only $2400, but his investment profits totaled about $45,000.

Carnegie stopped working for the railroad in 1865 and became a bond broker. Bond sales netted him handsome profits which he invested in iron and steel mills, and although he knew very little about the production processes he soon gained control of several factories turning out steel which was sold to manufacturers of wire, nails, cans, rails, bridges and other products. By the late 1800s Andrew Carnegie was a millionaire and a power in the world of iron and steel.

Then many of his customers decided to produce their own steel for making their fabricated products, and the Carnegie mills were threatened with serious competition. Carnegie was growing old, was not inclined to fight business rivals, had made his fortune and was prepared to retire.

One of the Carnegie competitors was the Federal Steel Company, organized with the financial backing of John Pierpont Morgan, a wealthy New York investment banker. In 1900 Morgan had a long talk with Charles M. Schwab, who had been brought up through the factory ranks by Andrew Carnegie and who was then president of the Carnegie Company. As a result of this conference Morgan bought the Carnegie properties for $492 million and subsequently established the United States Steel Corporation, which today has thirty-three subsidiary companies and continues to be a major power in the industrial world.

Today we are living in the age of steel, for steel is the basic metal underlying our mechanized society. To understand its importance, try to imagine what our world would be like if all the steel now in use were suddenly disintegrated. Skyscrapers and other buildings with steel skeletons would crash. Ocean liners, battleships and submarines would vanish from the seas. Automobiles would disappear from the highways and airplanes from the skies. The telephone, the telegraph, radio and television equipment and receivers would not exist. There would be no "tin" cans to hold foods and liquids, no industrial or agricultural tools or machines, no printing presses, no surgical instruments, no railroads, no guns or rockets or spacecraft —not even a needle or safety pin!

CHAPTER 9

Boom, Bust and Forward March!

One of the greatest get-rich-quick booms of all time exploded in January, 1848, when James W. Marshall found a gold nugget in a stream at Sutter's Mill in Coloma, California. News of the find spread like soft butter on hot bread, and immediately thousands of families left their homes and jobs in other parts of the country and headed westward pell-mell to dredge fortunes from the land and waters of California. The gold rush of the forty-niners was on in a big way.

Some of the prospectors struck it rich. Others found only useless hard work and poverty. Some men, however, reaped huge profits from the gold fields without going to California —they were the manufacturers of goods needed by the miners. Most of these manufacturers were in the industrial East, producing increased quantities of clothing, boots and shoes, picks and shovels, hats, wagons, tents and other merchandise. Baby cradles were in great demand—not for lulling infants to sleep, but to be used as "rockers" to wash sand away in sluices and leave gold dust, if any.

New England shipping companies made fortunes from

cargoes of all kinds of merchandise loaded aboard clipper ships bound round the Horn for California.

A few years later, still during the search for gold, a Philadelphia man who prospected around Pike's Peak in Colorado, made himself a wide-brimmed beaver hat to keep the rays of the hot sun off his head and face. A cowboy offered him five dollars for the hat, and he sold it. When he finally returned to Philadelphia he established a successful industry of his own by making "ten-gallon" hats which became popular in the West. He was John B. Stetson, a name still famous in the billion-dollar hatmaking business.

"Gold fever" was not confined to the United States. The news was carried by sailors to far places, and soon Chinese, Irishmen, Scandinavians and people of other nationalities flocked across the seas to California. A boomtown grew overnight with more tents and ramshackle huts than houses and was called San Francisco. There was little order and practically no law except what a man made with his own fists or gun.

President Zachary Taylor, recognizing the need for orderly government in the lawless territory, told the people of California and New Mexico (ceded to the United States as a result of the Mexican War) that they would be wise to draft state constitutions as a first step toward applying for admission to the Union. The Californians and New Mexicans accepted the suggestion, wrote constitutions and elected officials to enforce their provisions.

These actions had both good and bad effects. Orderly government was good. Law enforcement was good. But both constitutions provided that slavery would not be permitted in the territories, and this exclusion made the proslavery politicians in Washington very bitter. Some southerners who had migrated to California and New Mexico already owned slaves there. If the territories were admitted as "free" states, slavery would be abolished. When the President urged Congress to admit both to the Union no matter what their slavery policies were, the proslavery politicians made strenuous objections and even threatened secession from the Union of the states they represented.

With the gold rush at its peak, Congress enacted the "Compromise of 1850," under which California came into the Union as a free state, with the new territories of New Mexico and Utah awaiting admission. According to the compromise these territories, if and when they became states, could permit slavery or not, according to their own constitutions. This so-called popular sovereignty stirred up added bitterness between proslavery and antislavery groups and made it more evident that the slavery issue was a growing sore that would be hard to heal.

Many manufacturers in the industrial Northeast were too busy raking in money to give more than passing concern to the slavery question. They were producing more factory-made goods than ever, expecting to serve the increasing demands of people in new towns built near railroads in the West.

In 1840 railroads had less than 3000 miles of track in the United States. By 1856 there were about 25,000 miles of track in all directions, with more to come. Thousands of men found work on the railroads and in railroad shops. Shareholders received handsome profits from the railroad companies. Factories and towns were expected to spring up along the rights-of-way.

In 1854 Great Britain, Turkey and France joined forces against Russia in the Crimea to prevent Russia from dominating southeastern Europe, and the war brought urgent requests to the United States for huge quantities of food and supplies. This was a boon to western and southern farmers and cattle raisers and to northern manufacturers, because the sale of livestock, cotton, farm and factory-made products jumped their incomes to new highs, and the shipping companies whose vessels carried food and goods overseas were also getting richer.

Speculators bought up land near railroads, or where they thought railroads would be, and sold it to eager settlers at exorbitant prices. Whole cities were laid out on paper by shady characters who sold lots on promises that would never be kept. Storekeepers closed up shop, farmers left their farms, lawyers deserted their offices to get in on the land deals. Many mortgaged or sold homes and belongings to raise money to invest. The cost of food, clothing, and necessities skyrocketed in the boomtowns. The whole country was as inflated as its currency, and credit was easy to get.

In 1856 the Treaty of Paris ended the Crimean War, and the big food and cloth orders from Europe slacked off. The farmers and ranchers had more food on hand than normal markets could use, and the industrialists had stockpiles of cloth and other goods which they couldn't sell.

In August, 1857, the Ohio Life Insurance and Trust Company went out of business. This multimillion-dollar institution had been considered a symbol of strength and security, and its sudden and unexpected failure panicked the financial world. As yet there was no national banking system, and many unsound banks and business houses closed their doors or refused to make payments in gold or silver. In Philadelphia the Bank of Pennsylvania agreed to pay withdrawals in coin, and from

eleven o'clock in the morning until three o'clock in the afternoon on a single day it paid out almost two million dollars.

Fear and alarm invaded towns and cities. Several railroad
companies and other corporations went bankrupt because they
had overexpanded. Thirty to forty thousand desperate people
milled about Wall Street in New York, spreading rumors,
hearing new wild tales and seeking vainly for some miracle to
avoid utter ruin. Fortunes were swept away like dust before a
broom. Stores tried to sell merchandise "below wholesale
prices," but customers stayed away. Factories closed down,
farmers had no markets for crops, canal boats had little or
nothing to haul, and existing railroads carried few passengers
and not much freight. Thousands of people were thrown out
of work and could not pay their debts.

One business which did improve while others went to the
wall was that of fortunetelling. Palmists and clairvoyants were
besieged by worried customers anxious for a look into their
futures!

Although "The Great Panic" of 1857 soon lost its momen-
tum, it left an economic depression which lasted for a long
time.

Railroads were among the first to recover, and in 1859 Congress authorized construction of a railroad that would reach
from the East to the West Coast. Thousands of men returned
to work on the road, other businesses began to pick up slowly
—then, on August 29, 1859, a rich new force gushed into the
Industrial Revolution. Edwin L. Drake drilled the first oil
well.

Within a year a thousand more wells were sunk in Pennsylvania, and it wasn't long before the "black gold" was being
pumped out of West Virginia, Kentucky, Ohio, California
and other states. Then came the Civil War.

The Civil War was caused, in part at least, by the Industrial Revolution. The emphasis in the industrial North was on more machines, more factories, more products. The agricultural South grew more cotton (seven-eighths of the world supply), tobacco and rice and demanded more slaves to work the plantations. Politicians fought over the question of whether or not the new territories of Kansas and Missouri would become slave or free states. The smoldering slavery issue was beginning to blaze.

In 1858 the Republican presidential nominee, Abraham Lincoln, said, "A house divided against itself cannot stand. I believe this government cannot endure permanently half slave and half free. . . . It will become all one thing or the other. . . ."

The Civil War began on April 12, 1861, when the army of the newly formed Confederate States of America opened a bombardment of Fort Sumter in Charleston Harbor.

The war created a terrific manufacturing surge in the industrial North. Textile and flour mills, shoe factories, iron foundries and tanneries were going full blast. Most of the nation's railroads were in the North, affording fast transportation of war supplies and troops. The South, on the other hand, needed to import many manufactured goods for which it could pay in cotton, but an effective northern blockade made such exchanges virtually impossible.

The war ended with victory for the North in 1865 and a period of reconstruction began. Once again the Union was whole, but in the defeated South fire and firearms had left cities in ruins, destroyed farmlands and homes, brought normal business to a standstill and wrecked the southern economy. Slavery was outlawed, and although Negroes continued to live in what had been the Confederacy, most of them looked upon freedom as freedom to loaf. The plantation owners had little or no help to plant and harvest their cotton, tobacco, sugar cane and rice.

Northern "carpetbaggers," filled with hatred and greed, invaded the Southern states, controlled state and city reconstruction governments, and used all kinds of unscrupulous methods to cheat landowners and businessmen out of their holdings.

The Union Army sent soldiers to rebuild southern railroads, bridges, and to make debris-strewn canals and rivers fit for transportation again. A "Freedmen's Bureau" sought to provide education for Negroes and find employment for them. By borrowing money many Southern planters restored their lands, but others saw reasons to quit the growing of crops and turn to manufacturing. Northern industry and northern capital had contributed greatly to the Northern victory, and if a vigorous, strong South was to rise from the ashes of the war it seemed reasonable to believe that industry would accomplish such a feat more effectively than agriculture could.

Since cotton and tobacco were two of the South's greatest assets, the industrial-minded southerners began to build new plants where the cotton could be spun into thread and the thread made into cloth, and where the tobacco could be processed ready for smoking. In other words, the South began to combine its agriculture with a new and promising industrial program.

The rebuilding of Southern railroads became part of an expanding rail transportation era. With the coming of peace, work on the transcontinental and other railroads was resumed. The Central Pacific Railroad Company laid track Eastward from California; the Union Pacific headed Westward from St. Louis, Missouri. This was an undertaking of great magnitude, considering that the roadbed was dug with picks and shovels by thousands of men who also laid 110,000 tons of iron rails with 2 million bolts, 15 million spikes, 3½ million cross-ties and uncounted millions of feet of timber used for bridges and culverts. They fought desert heat, mountain cold, hostile Indians and other obstacles all the way, reaching a grand climax as the two roads were joined on May 10, 1869, at Promontory Point, Utah.

The nation was now welded together with rails of steel, with canals, rivers, lakes and roads, and all of these had a powerful impact upon the Industrial Revolution. Small factories expanded or merged into big companies to meet growing demands for goods which could be shipped with little difficulty at reasonable costs. Steamships not only plied the big rivers, but also sailed across the oceans, so that imports and exports increased.

A famous steamship also laid wire cable on the floor of the Atlantic Ocean, making it possible to telegraph messages between the United States and Europe. After two discouraging attempts that began in 1856 under the direction of Cyrus W. Field, the first cable link was completed in July, 1858, but three months later the insulation failed and no more messages could be carried.

In 1865 a 680-foot iron steamship, the *Great Eastern*, sailed from Valentia Harbor, Ireland, carrying 2500 miles of cable, to be unwound as the vessel sailed across the sea. After 1200 miles of cable had been paid out it broke in two and the *Great Eastern* turned back, but Cyrus Field was still persistent, and in July, 1866, the same ship undertook the same job again. This time there were no mishaps and the Atlantic cable stretched unbroken from Ireland to Newfoundland, bringing the New World into close touch with the Old. Now more than ever before, communication was playing an important part in the Industrial Revolution and in international and national relationships as well.

Up to this time communication in business correspondence had consisted of letters written in pen and ink, often by men employed for their handwriting clarity and skill. In 1867 Christopher L. Sholes, assisted by Carlos Glidden, Samuel W. Soulé and Matthias Schwalbach, designed and produced a "writing machine" in a small shop near Milwaukee, Wisconsin. The machine, which Sholes named the "Type Writer," had a series of lettered and numbered keys which, when struck with the fingers, printed letters or numbers on paper. Eventually the manufacture and sale of the device was undertaken by the firm of E. Remington and Sons, Ilion, New York, and one of the first customers to buy a typewriter was the famous author, Mark Twain. For advertising purposes he wrote a letter which the manufacturers printed and distributed. It said:

Gentlemen:
Please do not use my name in any way. Please do not even divulge the fact that I own a machine. I have entirely stopped using a Type-Writer for the reason that I never could write a letter with it to anybody without receiving a request by return mail that I would not only describe the machine, but state what progress I had made in the use of it, etc., etc. I don't like to write letters, and so I don't want people to know I own this curiosity-breeding little joker.
                    Yours truly, Saml L. Clemens.

The typewriter spelled out the beginning of another billion-dollar industry, and of a new kind of office worker—stenographers and typists.

Now it was possible for people to write neatly printed letters much faster than any penman could, to send them overland by coach or train and overseas by ship and, when speed was necessary, to rush words electrically over the "lightning wire." (The telegraph line had been completed from coast to coast in 1861.) The next big step was to make it possible for people to talk with each other by wire across long distances.

The step was completed by a Scotsman, Alexander Graham Bell, who lived in Boston, Massachusetts. A teacher of the deaf, Bell had experimented for some time to perfect what he called a "harmonic telegraph," by which he believed he could make an electric current carry sound through a wire. His trials were futile until one day in 1875, when his assistant, Thomas A. Watson, working on a transmitter in one room, accidentally touched metal to metal and made a tinkling sound which was heard by Bell on a receiver in another room.

Excitedly, Bell rushed to Watson's workroom to learn exactly what had happened. He discovered that the sound had been transmitted by a steady electric current, and that he and Watson had been on the wrong track by using an intermittent current similar to that used for the telegraph.

More experiments still failed to carry intelligible words over the wire, but on March 10, 1876, Bell was tinkering with a transmitter when he upset a bottle of acid, spilling some on his clothes. Instantly he cried out, "Mr. Watson, come here—I want you!"

Watson was in another room, but within a few seconds he rushed into Bell's workshop with a startling announcement. "Mr. Bell, I heard every word you said—distinctly!"

That was the historic birthday of the telephone, a marvelous instrument which has become as much a part of every office, factory, and business establishment as its furniture and machinery, and which is now a taken-for-granted instrument in millions of private homes.

Another invention developed in the mid-nineteenth century

was improved after the Civil War and led to the creation of one more big new industry—the manufacture of cameras and photographic accessories and film for home use and for motion pictures.

A pioneer in this field was Henry Fox Talbot, an Englishman, who in 1835 had put a lens in one end of a light-tight box, and paper coated with silver chloride at the other end. After pointing the lens at some external object and permitting light to strike the sensitized paper, he dipped the paper in a salt solution which washed away the silver chloride that had not been light-struck, thus leaving the image of the photographed object.

From this invention came an improvement called the "daguerreotype," conceived by Louis Jacques Mandé Daguerre and Joseph N. Niepce in France.

The man who perhaps deserves most of the credit for putting cameras into the hands of millions of men, women and children was George Eastman, born July 12, 1854, in Waterville, New York. As a twenty-year-old bank clerk in Rochester, Eastman saved money from his salary to invest in a camera and photographic equipment. Because the camera was big and cumbersome and required sensitized wet glass plates for the making of negatives, Eastman set out to simplify the whole process. After considerable experimenting he created dry glass plates which could be used much more easily than the wet kind, and he set up a shop for the making and selling of these plates.

In 1884 a man named William Walker devised a strip of sensitized paper which could be rolled up and used instead of the fragile glass plates. Using this principle, George Eastman designed and made a new kind of camera which he called a "Kodak" and sold for twenty-five dollars, fully loaded with a hundred-exposure film roll. When the owner had used the entire roll he brought the unopened camera to Eastman, who developed the film and reloaded the camera at a cost of ten dollars.

Five years later, in 1889, Eastman invented the first rolls of celluloid film, and in 1900 he produced a camera which was within the price range of almost everybody's pocketbook. This was the famous "Brownie," which sold for one dollar. Brownies were sold by the thousands, and the Eastman Kodak Company had launched another industry which was destined to become world-wide in scope.

As the Industrial Revolution affected more and more people in all walks of life, it was inevitable that new factories would be built, that industries would grow, that men and money would join forces with other men to make more money, and that there would be complaints, objections, strife and appeals for better working conditions by the workers who produced the manufactured goods.

Labor and capital were often in disagreement, and as industry itself became more complex, so did the labor-capital differences regarding wages and benefits. Today there are periodical and complicated "bargaining sessions" between management and labor, an outgrowth of simpler activity that began early in the nineteenth century, only a few years after the wheels of the Industrial Revolution started to roll.

No one can pinpoint the first times when groups of men in the same trade or calling banded together and paid dues to protect the secrets of their craft and control traffic in it. In the fifth century there were "Chiefs of Locksmiths" and bakers had a trade union as early as 630. Ancient records show that Europe had a "College of Fishermen" in 943 and a "Corporation of Butchers" in 1001. Fishermen, butchers, purse-

makers, tanners and shoemakers paid dues which were collected by the king, who granted the organizations certain
privileges in return.

In England the Industrial Revolution created labor evils
that later demanded labor reforms, many of which affected
the course of industry in America. American factory workers,
for instance, like those in Britain, often worked for twelve to
fourteen hours a day in badly ventilated, poorly lighted buildings. Many of the workers were children, some only eight or
ten years old. At the day's end the laborers trudged to their
homes, in many cases crowded tenements blackened on the
outside with soot from nearby smokestacks and as dismal and
gloomy as the murky factories themselves.

British legal restrictions were removed in 1825 to permit
the organization of labor groups, and several trade unions were
formed. Most of them broke up within a few months, and it
was not until 1845 that they began to revive and survive. As
the unions recruited more members and gathered strength, the
factory and mine owners decided to form associations of their
own to protect their interests. The result was a series of conflicts between labor and management. Some unions ordered
their members to stop work and strike for higher wages. Some
factory owners, in disputes with union leaders, shut down their
plants in what became known as "lockouts."

In the midst of the oppression and fights of the laboring
classes a German revolutionary and philosopher named Karl
Marx, living in Paris in 1843, advocated what he called "so-
cialism." In brief, Marx declared that the entire proletariat, or
working class, must reorganize society so that capitalism would
be overthrown. Under the Marxist philosophy the "workers
of the world" would share among themselves the results of

their labor, and all ownership of private property would be abolished.

In Paris Marx met Friedrich Engels. Together they made more attacks on capitalism and subsequently joined a German secret society known as "The League of the Just." Later this was changed to "The League of the Communists," and in 1847 Marx and Engels wrote a pamphlet, *Manifest der Kommunisten* (Communist Manifesto), which became famous as an exposition of the views of the Communist party concerning the working classes.

In 1864 Marx became the unofficial leader of the "International Working Men's Association" in London, a labor organization dedicated to overthrow capitalism. Known as the "First International," this association was symbolized by a bright red flag, and it was this symbol that inspired the term "Red" to describe revolutionists, anarchists and Communists.

While Marx was active in England, Americans were beginning to learn about labor organizations. Although union activities seemed best suited to factories and industrial workers, the American farmer realized that there was strength in numbers.

In 1867 a federal government employee named Oliver Kelley founded a fraternal organization for farmers, called "Patrons of Husbandry." This did not purport to be a union as such, but instead was a kind of lodge known as the "Grange," with secret ceremonies and with membership offered to farmers and their families.

Although the so-called Granger Movement could not foster strikes as an industrial labor union could, it recruited enough thousands of members to organize independent political parties which, hopefully, could influence public officials to sponsor or originate legislation that would be beneficial to farmers.

Industrially, however, the labor union was to become a prime factor in manufacturing in America.

In 1872 the International Working Men's Association moved its headquarters from London to New York City and soon sponsored the creation of a new labor union, the "United Workers of America," whose main cry was "Down With Capitalism!"

The United Workers of America in 1874 was one of few labor unions in America. Others had preceded it, but had died out for various reasons. One that did survive was "The Noble Order of the Knights of Labor," which was formed in 1869 in Philadelphia, Pennsylvania, by Uriah Smith Stevens, a clothing worker. This order existed for several years as a secret fraternal body, complete with mystic rites and passwords, but in 1873 another financial panic crippled business and commerce, and the Knights of Labor came into the open. In 1877 it helped to engineer strikes against coal mines and railroads and recruited hundreds of new members, including many farmers. By 1878 it had established "local assemblies" in seven states and was the foremost labor group in the country. In 1880 it launched a crusade designed to organize *all* workers in every trade and profession, and also to revise the banking system and economic policies of the government.

By that time, especially because of the boom period after the Civil War, the Industrial Revolution had taken a firm hold in the United States and factory-made goods made up about 65 per cent of the nation's industrial output, worth almost five and a half million dollars.

An internal struggle began between Knights of Labor who believed that their organization should include all kinds of workers, and Knights who argued that the various craft unions that made up the order should have the right to deal independently with employers; for example, members who worked in shoe factories would deal directly with their factory owners, those in clothing factories would deal with their own bosses, and so on.

This split caused several craft unions to withdraw from the Knights of Labor in December, 1886, and to create a new organization, the American Federation of Labor (AFL), through which they would work as independent crafts. The AFL brought in more and more unions and within a few years became strong enough to bring about the eight-hour workday in American industry.

The labor movement made both gains and losses in the first quarter of the twentieth century. A Department of Labor was created in the federal government in 1913, giving labor a voice in the President's Cabinet. New laws were enacted to restrict certain legal moves of employers against the unions and to provide shorter working hours for railroad workers.

Throughout the 1920s, after several legal and internal squabbles, the labor unions suffered financial gains and losses, and during the great economic depression that began in 1929 union members resigned in droves.

In 1935 the leaders of eight AFL unions created the Committee for Industrial Organization (CIO), headed by beetle-browed John L. Lewis of the United Mine Workers. This group invaded mass-production industries in an effort to convert craft unions into industrial unions, and when Lewis and his associates succeeded in weaning ten unions away from the AFL, the latter expelled the ten and blamed them for weakening the labor cause.

Within three years the Committee for Industrial Organization changed its name to the Congress of Industrial Organizations and had recruited some thirty-two international unions in the fields of automobile manufacturing, iron and steel production, shipping, electrical products and the manufacture of rubber.

From 1938 to 1940 there were numerous strikes, but with the entry of the United States into World War II the labor organizations promised to keep strikes to a minimum and to devote full efforts to national defense industries. At that time the unions' membership totaled about 14,000,000.

As soon as the war ended another series of strikes began, and some members of Congress considered that the growing power of the unions was a national danger. In 1947 the legislators passed the Labor Management Relations Act (the "Taft-Hartley Law"), designed to pull some of the claws of the labor tiger.

Membership and activities of the unions and the farm Granges affected not only the social and economic conditions of the country, but its political future as well. With millions of workers' and farmers' votes at stake, candidates for public office—federal, state, county and municipal—adopted platforms and made promises which they hoped would attract the farm and labor vote, a technique which politicians continue to use and probably will for a long time to come.

In 1948 and 1949 dissension broke out in the CIO ranks. One "right-wing" faction was strongly opposed to Communism, while a "left-wing" group criticized the "imperialism" of the United States and seemed to favor certain principles of the Communist party. In a wide rift that followed, several of the left-wing units were expelled from the CIO.

Eventually the AFL and the CIO patched up many of their differences and joined forces as the AFL-CIO. Although alleged corruption in labor organizations led to congressional investigations which exposed widespread irregularities, the trade unions continue to call strikes, and in fact they maintain the power to paralyze the entire industrial output of the nation if they choose to do so.

Two major industries in which unionism plays a vital part are those involving the manufacture of automobiles and aircraft, but in the days when the automobile was the novel "horseless carriage" and the aircraft was only a "motor-driven box kite" the only labor problems were those of the few men whose genius made these machines work. Both inventions heralded global expansion of the Industrial Revolution.

CHAPTER 10

Wheels and Wings

In a town with the quaint name of Stoke Poges in Buckinghamshire, England, is a church in which one stained-glass window has a design that is related more to the Industrial Revolution than to religion. It portrays a human figure straddling a wheeled contraption that was apparently propelled by the feet of the rider, who ran and sat, ran and sat.

This was the technique used in 1690 by a Frenchman who invented a crude two-wheeled vehicle called a *celerifere*, consisting of a wooden pole or beam with one front and one rear wheel. The rider sat astride the pole and moved the vehicle by pushing it with his feet, one on each side of the wheels. There was no steering device, and he also used his feet to control the direction of travel. It is quite possible that this was the original ancestor of the bicycle—and the bicycle has been called "the father of the automobile."

A few minor improvements produced the *velocifere* in 1789 and the *celeripede* in 1810, but the basic principles were about the same until Baron Karl Drais von Sauerbronn of Germany in 1816 invented a two-wheeled instrument, the *draisine*, that had a handlebar enabling the rider to turn the front wheel to right or left.

The baron's original idea was improved by various French, German and English inventors and by the baron himself, who in 1818 gave public exhibitions in which he ran-and-sat at speeds of perhaps five or six miles an hour. His machine had a fancy saddle and elbow rests. The demonstrations aroused popular interest in the vehicle, but its manufacture was expensive and only a few wealthy people (such as the prince regent and other "dandies") could afford one, a fact that led others to call it the "dandy horse."

The "dandy horse" fad spread to the United States but soon lost popularity, and it was not until 1839 that this mode of travel won new interest. In that year a Scot named Kirkpatrick MacMillan, using a dandy horse as a basis, invented pedals and cranks that enabled a rider to sit on a comfortable seat and propel the vehicle by "pumping" the pedals.

MacMillan rode about the countryside on his vehicle for several years, and on at least one occasion was arrested and fined for "furious driving."

In 1846 Gavin Dalzell made several improvements in Mac-Millan's device and manufactured and sold a great many "Dalzells."

To MacMillan and Dalzell goes the major share of credit for creating the basic vehicle that became today's bicycle. In later years more improvements were made—pedals with rotary cranks, big front and small rear wheels, chain drives, spokes of wire instead of wood, coaster brakes, rubber tires and ball bearings.

In 1869 Sylvester H. Roper of Roxbury, Massachusetts, invented a steam-driven bicycle which was featured for several years at circuses and fairs. Advertising posters described it as

"The only Steam Velocipede in the World. Pronounced a perfect triumph in mechanism. It can be driven up any hill and will outspeed any horse in the world." This, perhaps, was the forerunner of the motorcycle.

The popularity of bicycles spread from Europe to the United States and led to the founding of a bicycle factory by Colonel Albert A. Pope in Boston, Massachusetts, in 1877.

Bicycles became very popular in America, and in the 1890s there were some 250 bicycle manufacturers in the United States, representing a sixty-million-dollar industry which provided the average family with a means of travel that did not require horses for power. The most important contribution of these machines to the Industrial Revolution, however, was in achieving a major improvement in roads through insistent demands of bicycle riders. In many towns and cities riders organized cycling clubs, and on week ends or vacations they "wheeled" in large groups to other towns or to picnic areas or resorts; but the local roads were so muddy or rutty or bumpy that there was often little pleasure in the riding.

One by one the local clubs began to join a national organization known as "The League of American Wheelmen," and with its large and growing membership the League acquired enough influence to begin what it called the "Good Roads Movement." It lodged official complaints with congressmen and local politicians and kept up such a barrage of demands for improved roads that in 1893 the federal government set up a new Office of Roads Inquiry to work with states and counties to build better roads.

Better roads were important to cyclists, stagecoach lines, wagon freight lines and farmers, but just at the time that the Office of Roads Inquiry was created, two brothers built a machine that was destined to make paved roads a necessity and to bring about the building of the greatest highway system in the world. The machine was the automobile. The brothers were Charles and Frank Duryea of Canton, Illinois.

Although the Duryeas were among the pioneer automobile makers in the United States they were actually trailing certain European inventors. The origin of the very first internal combustion engine (that is, an engine operated by exploding gases) seems to be in doubt. Some authorities claim that the first such engine was built in 1820 by W. Cecil, who described it in detail at a meeting of the Cambridge (England) Philosophical Society. Others say that the Dutch scientist, Christiaan Huygens, designed an internal combustion engine in 1678, to be operated with gunpowder, but never built one; and that the first practical engine of this kind, using illuminating gas, was built about 1860 by Étienne Lenoir, a Frenchman.

Whatever the true origin, it appears that internal combustion engines were used in Europe in 1866 as motive power for tricycles or carriages by a pair of German engineers, Eugen Langen and Nikolaus Otto; in 1885 by Gottlieb Daimler; and in 1886 by Karl Benz.

In the United States on May 8, 1879, George B. Selden had applied for a patent on a four-wheeled carriage powered by an internal combustion engine. Because he kept making improvements that required frequent amendments to his application, the patent itself was not formally issued until November 5, 1895, and at that time it was the first patent ever issued for such a machine.

It was 1891 when Charles Duryea saw a Langen-Otto engine in operation and decided that it could be used to propel a vehicle. Duryea knew little or nothing about Selden's work or the European developments in this field, and with his brother Frank he set out independently to build a gasoline-powered carriage. When it was completed in 1892 it weighed seven hundred pounds, looked like a buggy without a horse and was called a "buggyaut." The motor was under the seat.

When trials showed that the vehicle was practicable the Duryeas opened the Duryea Motor Wagon Company in Springfield, Massachusetts, to make "buggyauts." It was a small beginning for what became an American industrial giant —the manufacture of automobiles.

The Duryeas were not the only Americans experimenting with horseless carriages. An engineer named Charles B. King made vehicles similar to those of the Duryeas, and at about the same time Elwood Haynes of Portland, Indiana, built his own version and for many years afterward headed a company which made and sold "Haynes" automobiles. In June, 1896, a tall, rangy machinist rode through the streets of Detroit in a gasoline-driven vehicle which he called an "autocycle." Although he may not have known it, he was riding into fame and riches on an invention that was soon to pull the world out of a rut and change the way of life for millions of his fellow Americans. His name was Henry Ford.

Born in 1863 on a Wayne County, Michigan, farm, Henry Ford grew into boyhood with a hearty dislike for pitching hay, milking cows, plowing fields or doing other ordinary farm chores. He much preferred to help a blacksmith make horseshoes or to sharpen saws or fix broken farm tools for friends and neighbors. He was fascinated by any kind of machinery, eager to study its wheels, gears or other parts to learn what they did and how they did it. When he was only twelve years old he was taking apart and repairing broken clocks and watches for the fun he got out of such work.

His father, William Ford, often found fault with Henry for his failure to take an interest in the farm, and arguments between father and son became so frequent and bitter that the boy left home when he was sixteen and got a job as an apprentice machinist in the Detroit Dry Dock Company. He worked ten hours a day, seven days a week. His pay was $2.50 a week.

When he completed his apprenticeship in 1882 he spent a year setting up and repairing Westinghouse steam-driven road engines in southern Michigan, and it was then that he began to think about building a steam-powered farm tractor which could replace the horse for plowing. After several experiments he made such a tractor, using kerosene to fire the boiler, and he reached two conclusions: first, that because a tractor must have a light, high-pressure boiler, it would be dangerous to the user; and second, even if he developed a workable tractor it would have to be sold at a high price to produce a profit, and would therefore appeal to a very limited market.

Ford now discontinued the tractor project and began to dream about a carriage propelled by an internal combustion engine, a vehicle that could be made and sold at a reasonable price and used for many purposes by farmers and others.

In 1892, while working as an engineer for the Edison Illuminating Company of Detroit (now the Detroit Edison Company) he heard and read about the Duryea brothers' "buggyaut," and he decided to explore the field of internal combustion.

In a woodshed behind his Detroit home on Bagley Avenue he spent almost all of his spare time tinkering. Every night, every weekend his neighbors saw and heard him puttering around his home workshop, and when it became known that he was trying to build a one-cylinder gasoline engine some of the townsfolk nicknamed him "Crazy Ford."

Henry couldn't care less. He finished the little engine and

brought it from the woodshed to the kitchen of his home, where he put it on a small table and prepared to start it. As his wife Clara looked on, Henry set the machine in operation. It coughed and sputtered and made a tremendous racket, but it is probable that Henry Ford paid little attention to the noise because the thrill and excitement of seeing his invention burst into life must have drowned out all mere sounds.

Now that he knew how to build a workable engine, Ford set out to make one with two cylinders and power enough to move a carriage. When the engine was finished, he designed and built a carriage in which to install it. Instead of using wooden-spoke buggy wheels as the Duryeas had done, he mounted a light frame on four bicycle wheels, attached the engine to the frame and rigged a belt drive from the motor to the rear wheels. The first Ford automobile was completed in the quiet hours after midnight in June, 1896.

When Ford, excited and anxious, started to roll the horseless carriage out of his workshop he discovered that it was wider than the door! In his eagerness for a trial run he chopped out part of the shed wall and took the vehicle out on the deserted street. It was raining hard, but probably a hurricane would not have kept Henry Ford from taking his first ride in his four-wheeled triumph. He started the engine and drove up one street and down another for perhaps half a mile or more, while along the route sleepy people poked their heads out of windows to see what was making all the commotion.

The success of his "car" overshadowed Ford's other activities, including his job as chief engineer for the Edison Illuminating Company, and he continued to experiment with internal combustion engines and built two improved vehicles. In 1899 his employer suggested that he devote more time to his daily work and less to his horseless carriages, so on August 19,

1899, he resigned and, with a group of financial backers, organized the Detroit Automobile Company, with himself as its chief engineer.

It appears that his backers wanted two things—automobiles that would sell for high prices to wealthy customers, and publicity that would help make the sales. The first was not unusual, for cars were made by hand, were expensive and were considered to be "playthings" for rich people only.

The second, publicity, came with speed. Henry Ford designed and built several racing cars, one of which he drove to victory in a contest with Alexander Winton, another automobile manufacturer, at Grosse Pointe, Michigan, on October 10, 1901. At another time he whizzed to more fame at the then incredible speed of seventy miles per hour, and on January 12, 1904, he set a world's record of 39.4 seconds for the mile, driving his famous "No. 999" across the frozen surface of Lake St. Clair.

Since cars were a rich man's luxury, sales were not made in overwhelming numbers, but in 1899, when Ford organized the Detroit Automobile Company, another inventor had designed and built a one-cylinder engine mounted on a two-seater carriage that could travel about eighteen miles an hour. His name was Russell E. Olds and his contraption was called the "Oldsmobile."

Russell Olds has been called the "Father of Automobile Mass Production." Taking a cue from Eli Whitney's mass production of firearms, Olds had his engines produced by Horace and John Dodge in their machine shop, his transmissions made by Henry Leland (who later produced the Cadillac), the carriage bodies somewhere else. All were delivered to a central point where they were put together on the first automotive "assembly line." Even more important was the fact that the Oldsmobile sold for about five hundred dollars, bringing the cost within the range of the average middle-class family.

Automobiles were not yet universally popular. They frightened both horses and people and were considered by man to be a public nuisance and hazard. One man, Uriah Smith, of Battle Creek, Michigan, built a "Horsey Horseless Carriage" which had a life-size reproduction of a horse's head and neck attached to its front as a kind of decoy to keep live horses from being terrorized on the road!

According to some newspapers the automobile was merely a fad that would soon die out. It was this prediction that died out, however, because more and more automobile factories came into being in the early years of the twentieth century.

Henry Ford's Detroit Automobile Company went bankrupt in 1901, but Ford refused to quit, and on June 16, 1903, he helped to organize the Ford Motor Company. As president of the company he owned only 25.5 per cent of its stock, but in later years he and his son Edsel bought up shares owned by minority stockholders for more than $105 million and became sole owners of the company.

Recognizing the value of and need for an inexpensive car, Ford produced a "Fordmobile runabout" to sell for about eight hundred dollars. It was also known as "Model A" and became the first of several alphabetical designations used by the company—Model K, Model N, Model R, Model S.

In 1907, using improved mass production methods, the Ford Motor Company unveiled its first "Model T," an automobile which Henry Ford himself described as a "motor car for the great multitude." He was right, for the Model T, simple in appearance and in operation, rugged enough for town or country, sold for less than a thousand dollars and put the

American family on the road. Sales jumped, Ford built new factories, and within a few years his cars were rolling off the assembly lines by the thousands.

Other manufacturers began to produce cars at various price levels, and the horse-drawn buggy gradually became a museum piece. The great industrial enterprise created by the genius of Henry Ford, the Duryeas, Haynes, Olds, the Dodge brothers, Leland, David Buick and many other pioneers has had a profound and lasting influence upon the social, economic and cultural values of our time.

Consider, for example, that this book was written in 1963, just one hundred years after Henry Ford was born. When he was a baby the population of the United States was largely rural, and about 60 per cent of all employed persons earned their living by farming. There were less than one hundred cities with more than eight thousand residents. The horse provided the farmer's transportation as well as the motive power for his farm implements.

A family located more than twelve miles from a railroad lived in an isolation broken only by an occasional traveler or a weekly trip to town for provisions. Wagon trains lumbered westward carrying homesteaders into unclaimed land at a speed averaging fifteen miles a day, a strong contrast to the jet-age travel of the 1960s.

Henry Ford died on April 7, 1947, at his home, Fair Lane, in Dearborn, Michigan, as the result of a cerebral hemorrhage. He was eighty-three years old. By that time the majority of Americans were living in cities and suburbs. Trucks, tractors and modern farm implements had multiplied the efficiency of the farmer to a point where only 7 per cent of the working population supplied food and other farm products for the rest of the nation.

Today the automobile, the truck and the tractor have become necessities to the American way of life. In 1963 more than 75 million motor vehicles were in daily use on the country's 3½ million miles of roads and city streets, and work was progressing on a great network of superhighways. Thanks to the automobile, few families now are more than minutes away from their neighbors, their work and the shops of busy communities.

Henry Ford's vision was a seed of change. His determination to "build a motorcar for the great multitude" led to the serious development of mass production in the automotive industry and to a new kind of social and industrial revolution that changed American life and still echoes throughout the world.

In 1963 the chairman of the board of directors of the Ford Motor Company was Henry Ford II, forty-six-year-old grandson of the founder. The company has factories not only in the United States but also in England, Canada, Australia, West Germany, Brazil, Argentina and Mexico, with subsidiaries in several other countries. As this book is written, the latest (1962) annual report of the company shows that world-wide sales of Ford cars, trucks and tractors for that year totaled 3,376,138 and were increasing. Undoubtedly the "great multitude" envisioned by Henry Ford is even greater than he ever imagined it would be.

When Henry Ford, the Duryeas and other inventors were studying internal combustion engines and thinking about building horseless carriages, pioneers in another field of transportation were looking skyward and studying the flight of birds.

In the 1890s, when bicycles were at the peak of their popularity, two brothers made a living in a shop in Dayton, Ohio, where they sold and repaired the two-wheelers. The brothers were Wilbur and Orville Wright, and their dreams, perseverance and genius were to lift them literally to the heights; but others had helped to show the way.

For centuries earth-bound man watched the graceful movements of birds on the wing and sought to imitate them. More than two thousand years before Christ there were legends about men who flew or could fly. One tells of King Bladud, whose twenty-year reign of England began in 863 B.C. Bladud was a necromancer, a magician, who had been educated in Greece and who founded the city of Bath. It was there that he invented a set of wings covered with feathers and declared that he would fly through the air like an eagle. He climbed to the top of a tower, fastened the wings to his arms and looked down upon his awe-struck subjects awaiting the performance of his greatest feat of magic. The result was described in writing by Geoffrey of Monmouth in A.D. 1147:

> Bathe was by Bladud to perfection brought.
> By Necromanticke Arts, to flye he sought:
> As from a Towre he thought to scale the Sky,
> He brake his neck, because he soar'd too high.

King Bladud plummeted to his death upon the Temple of Apollo, "striving to play the Fowle or the Foole."

Many adventurous men died seeking the secret of flight, but many others continued the search. On June 5, 1783, two brothers, Joseph and Jacques Montgolfier, of Annonay, France, made a globe of linen 105 feet in circumference and suspended it above a small fire in which chopped straw was used as fuel. The huge cloth bag filled out and soon rose into the air, floated high in the sky for some ten minutes and drifted to a landing nearly two miles distant. This was the first successful balloon flight, and it led to more experiments by the Montgolfiers and others.

The first living passengers to be hauled aloft by a balloon were a sheep, a rooster and a duck. Their flight took place September 19, 1783, at Versailles, in a cage suspended beneath a Montgolfier balloon.

The next month, October 15, Jean François Pilâtre de Rozier, of Metz, became the first human balloonist, and after his successful flight in a captive balloon there was a procession of similar flights and improvements in the lighter-than-air vessels.

The greatest difficulty about balloons was that once in the air they were at the mercy of air currents and could not be steered. Scores of inventions designed to overcome this obstacle were not successful until 1875, when a German engineer named Paul Haenlein built and flew a cigar-shaped balloon which was propelled by an internal combustion engine. This was the ancestor of the later Zeppelin.

Balloon flights excited the interest of children, and a nine-year-old English boy, George Cayley, was one who made toy balloons of paper, inflated with hot air from lighted candles. Later, however, Cayley made bird-shaped kites which flew as gliders, and in 1849 one of these actually carried a boy through the air for a short distance, a flight which may have been a first of its kind.

More than forty years after this incident, in 1891, a German named Otto Lilienthal was eager to ferret out the secrets of controlled flight. He studied birds as they soared through the air, studied the action of wind on wing surfaces of kites and read everything he could find that related to flying. He built a glider, then constructed a high cone-shaped mound of earth so that he could take his ship to the top and launch it into the wind from any direction.

In flight he steered his fragile craft by shifting his body from side to side or back and forth. His glider was a success and he proceeded to build others with new and improved features. In the five years following that first flight in 1891 he flew more than two thousand times. Deciding that the next important step was powered flight, in 1896 he planned to install a small motor on a special glider. Before doing so he decided to make an ordinary glide in the ship. The launching was made in the teeth of a high wind, and moments later the aircraft was buffeted upward, nose first, then crashed to the ground. Lilienthal died the next day from a broken back.

Lilienthal's many successful flights had been publicized around the world, and pictures of him and his gliders found their way into the bicycle shop of the Wright brothers in Dayton. From early childhood the Wrights had been interested in flying. Like other boys they often made and flew kites of all kinds and sizes, and as they became more and more fascinated by the glider experiments of Lilienthal, Octave Chanute and other pioneers, they built bigger and bigger kites. When Wilbur and Orville agreed that they should try to fly in a glider of their own manufacture, they made what was really a huge box kite. Its double wings were eighteen feet long, five feet wide.

To get such a giant into the air the Wrights knew they must have a strong wind, so they asked the Weather Bureau to name areas where high winds blew steadily.

"The beaches in North Carolina can provide all the wind you want," the Weather Bureau said.

To North Carolina they went, to a place called Kill Devil Hill, near Kitty Hawk. There in October, 1900, they assembled their biplane-glider. At first they flew it unmanned like a kite, to test its airworthiness. Then they launched it with one man lying prone, working the controls with his feet.

They learned much from their first flights and when they returned to Dayton they drew plans for a second glider, larger than the first. This they took back to Kill Devil Hill in July, 1901, for more experiments, some of which revealed new information about the action of air on man-made wings. Back in Dayton they built a wind tunnel to make further studies, which led to the construction of a third glider with a thirty-two-foot wingspread, in which they subsequently made more than a thousand successful glides.

Now the Wrights believed they knew enough about heavier-than-air craft to install an engine in a glider and make powered flights. Their wind tunnel and other tests convinced them that they must have an eight-horsepower engine to make their airplane fly. They designed the engine themselves and had it built, along with a wooden propeller, by their own machinist, C. E. Taylor.

They shipped the engine and propeller to Kitty Hawk in September, 1903, together with a new aircraft whose wings measured 40 by 6½ feet. After successful tests of the ship as a glider they laid a long, single wooden track, covered with iron, on a slope not far from their camp.

Stormy weather delayed the great powered-flight adventure, but on December 17, 1903, the time was at hand. On that bitter cold and blustery Thursday morning the machine was placed on the monorail track, headed into the wind. Orville lay face down on the center of the lower wing as the motor was started and allowed to warm up for a few minutes. Then came the thrilling moment when he released the wire that held back the plane. Slowly it began to roll along the track, with

Wilbur running alongside. Seconds later the ship rose from the rail and flew against a 21-mile wind at a speed of about 30 miles an hour. It landed only 120 feet away, but that short distance marked one of the greatest events in world history—the success of powered flight.

Later that same day the brothers made two more flights, one of 195 feet, another of 852 feet.

The airplane was here to stay, and the success at Kitty Hawk signaled the beginning of an aviation industry that was to revolutionize transportation and warfare, provide world-wide employment for millions of men and women, and open the way for the scientific exploration of limitless space.

Space exploration, however, owes much to pioneers in fields far removed from flight itself, pioneers whose discoveries and achievements helped to lead the world into another revolution of which you and I are now a part—whether we like it or not!

CHAPTER 11

Talking Tin Foil, Rays and War

The pricking of a finger inspired a remarkable discovery by one of the world's greatest inventors, Thomas Alva Edison. This is how he described the event:

I was singing to the mouthpiece of a telephone when the vibrations of the wire sent the fine steel point into my finger. That set me to thinking. If I could record the action of the point, and then send the point over the same surface afterward, I saw no reason why the thing would not talk. I tried the experiment, first on a strip of telegraph paper, and found that the point made an alphabet. I shouted the word "Halloo! Halloo!" into the mouthpiece, ran the paper back over the steel point, and heard a faint "Halloo! Halloo!" in return. That's the whole story. The discovery came through the pricking of a finger.

Edison made a rough sketch on a piece of paper which he handed to John Kruesi, a machinist in his shop.

"Make this up, will you?" Edison said. On the paper was a notation, "$18," the estimated cost of producing the machine.

"What's it for?" Kruesi asked.

"It's a talking machine," Edison answered.

154

"Oh, sure," the machinist said, laughing.

When the pieces were made and assembled, the device was placed on Edison's desk. One feature was a tin-foil covered cylinder close to a small needle, and another was a horn, like a megaphone. Edison adjusted the needle so that it touched the tin foil; then he turned a crank which made the cylinder revolve, and at the same time he spoke loudly into the horn: "Mary had a little lamb, its fleece was white as snow." As he spoke he watched the needle move along and scratch the tinfoil, while Kruesi looked on.

Edison returned the needle to the end of the cylinder and again turned the crank. This time his voice came out of the horn, repeating, "Mary had a little lamb . . ."

In this way, in 1878, a pricked finger, a "Halloo!" and part of a nursery rhyme introduced the "talking machine" which grew into today's high-fidelity and stereophonic record players.

In 1883, some four years after Edison produced the first successful electric light bulb, he noticed in continued experiments that a coating of carbon smudged the inside surfaces of the glass globes, except for a fine, clear line shaped like the connection that held the carbon filament. Why, why, why?

To find the answer he inserted a small piece of copper (an "electrode") near, but not touching, the filament in the bulb and discovered that when he applied a positive electrical charge to the copper, a negative charge flowed to it from the filament.

This strange and unaccountable behavior was called "the Edison effect" and Edison patented it in 1883, but he was so busy with other inventions that he failed to explore it further.

While Edison continued to produce new creations—the dynamo, the storage battery, the movie projector among them—

a German physicist, Wilhelm Konrad von Roentgen, was studying the passage of electricity through gases in a Crookes tube and made an accidental discovery of great significance.

A Crookes tube, named for Sir William Crookes, an English physicist, was a pear-shaped glass bulb with metal plates sealed inside at top and bottom. When a strong electrical charge was sent into each plate the tube glowed, although there was no wire or other metal connection between the two plates. Crookes found that the glow was made by what he called "cathode rays," and another name for his invention was the cathode-ray tube.

One day in 1895 Professor von Roentgen was conducting experiments with a Crookes tube which he had covered with heavy cardboard. He happened to notice that a sheet of paper which had been coated with a chemical solution (barium-platino-cyanide) glowed with a greenish fluorescence. Although the paper was five or six feet away, he correctly guessed that this weird effect must be caused by the rays in the tube—and yet the tube was shielded with the cardboard!

As a further experiment he placed several thick books and stacks of paper between the tube and the coated sheet, but the strange green glow was still there. Holding one hand near the covered tube, von Roentgen was startled to see the shadows of the bones in his hand and fingers. Obviously some new and mysterious rays were coming from the tube, and since he did not know what they were he used the algebraic symbol for the unknown quantity to name them "X-rays."

The X-ray and the Edison effect were to make highly important contributions to the progress of modern science and industry.

In 1896, when von Roentgen announced his discovery to the world, a French physicist named Antoine Henri Becquerel was studying the fluorescent properties of various substances, one of which was a compound of uranium. It was generally known that certain materials would fluoresce, or glow, when they were exposed to light, especially sunlight. In the course of Becquerel's studies, however, storms arose and cloudy skies made him decide to postpone further work until the return of fair weather.

When the sun shone again Becquerel took his uranium and other materials from a desk drawer in which he had stored them. With no scientific purpose in mind he had placed the materials on top of several covered photographic negatives which were to be developed. He decided to process the negatives before resuming his current tests. He was somewhat upset to discover that one negative, when developed, appeared to be light-struck and therefore spoiled, but closer inspection revealed the shadowy outline of the container in which his uranium salt had been stored. Knowing about Roentgen's newly discovered X-rays, Becquerel wondered whether or not the uranium itself had projected the image. He deliberately placed the uranium on another unexposed negative and put both into a desk drawer.

The next day he found that the same thing had happened. After more experiments he established that uranium, even when it was not exposed to sunlight, emitted mysterious rays which could penetrate paper and metal, much in the way X-rays did. Becquerel's name for his discovery was "radioactivity."

As the nineteenth century neared its end many scientists were experimenting with X-rays and radioactive substances. Two who won lasting fame were Pierre and Marie Curie, both of whom studied physics at the University of Paris. They were married in 1895, and when Becquerel announced his studies of radioactivity the Curies worked as a team to conduct further experiments in this field.

Since the uranium used by Becquerel was obtained from pitchblende (a hard, black substance resembling hardened tar), the Curies decided to learn what other secrets pitchblende might hold. In 1898 they succeeded in extracting from it two wholly new elements—polonium (named for Marie Curie's native Poland) and radium.

For these discoveries the Curies, along with Antoine Henri Becquerel, were awarded the Nobel Peace Prize in 1903.

In 1906 Pierre Curie was run over by a horse-drawn cart in Paris and instantly killed. His widow carried on their work in radioactivity and took his place as head professor of physics at the University of Paris. Thanks to her genius and tireless work, the scientific world knows that radium can and does save human lives, and its controlled use has been of immeasurable value, especially in the treatment of cancer.

Ironically, this same radioactivity can be a killer, and one day the peoples of the world were to face the horrors of radioactive death-dust that could be showered upon them by terrible new weapons made possible by a growing knowledge of one of the smallest of all particles, the atom. This frightening future, however, was not to unfold completely until several years after the death of Marie Curie in 1934.

In the meantime other scientists were digging deeper into the mysteries of electricity. One of these explorers was a young Italian, Guglielmo Marconi, who was deeply impressed by a discovery of Heinrich Hertz, a German physicist, that an electric current produced invisible waves that sped through the air. In 1895, working at his home in Bologna, Italy, Marconi rigged up a crude antenna and telegraphic transmitter and succeeded in capturing an electrical signal over a distance of two miles without wires. He called his invention a "wireless."

After making various improvements and demonstrations Marconi accepted an invitation from the Italian government to equip its battleships with his invention, which made it possible for ships twelve miles apart to communicate with each other or with shore stations.

On December 12, 1901, Marconi climaxed his experiments by flying a kite to a height of four hundred feet on the coast of Newfoundland—but it was not an ordinary kite flight. The kite carried aloft a long, thin wire from which a connection extended to a receiving instrument in a small wooden shack on the ground.

At the same time, in the south of England, far across the Atlantic, one of Marconi's associates sat at a transmitter in a high tower and used a telegraph key to send the letter "S"—three dots—into the atmosphere. At the appointed hour Marconi sat at the receiver in the shack in Newfoundland with a set of earphones on his head, listening anxiously to see whether or not the electrical waves would carry the signal across the ocean.

He was nervous, impatient, almost discouraged. Was he wrong? Was his kite high enough? Was the equipment in good order? Had something broken down in the transmitter? Suddenly he sat bolt upright, both hands against the earphones. Wide-eyed, he snatched them off and almost threw them at an assistant.

"Take these," he said. "Tell me if you hear anything!"

The assistant listened intently, then gave a loud laugh that was almost a cheer. "I hear it!" he exclaimed. "I hear it! I hear the three clicks."

Marconi's accomplishments marked the beginning of what

we know as "radio," a term derived from the designation "radiotelegraph," which was given to Marconi's invention by the United States Navy.

While Marconi was doing his early experimentation in Italy, another scientific explorer, Sir Joseph John Thomson, proved in 1897 that cathode rays consisted of particles smaller than atoms, particles which were later given the name of *electrons*. Thomson pointed out that the so-called Edison effect, which Edison himself never followed up, was caused when the extremely hot filament in Edison's light bulb threw off electrons having negative charges which attracted them to the positively charged copper near the filament. This stream of electrons closed the circuit just as a wire might have done.

Studying Thomson's findings in 1904 another British physicist, Sir John Fleming, who had once worked for Edison, invented a vacuum tube similar to that which produced the Edison effect, except that he made a copper plate which surrounded the filament, and applied an alternating electric current (AC) to the plate. This current, alternating swiftly between positive and negative, attracted electrons from the filament at each positive impulse and repelled them at each negative impulse. The result was that the tube produced a current which flowed only in one direction—a direct current (DC). Since it rectified, or changed, AC to DC, it was called a "rectifier." It was also known as a "diode" (from the Greek meaning "two-way") because it had only two main parts, the filament and the plate. The diode was capable of detecting wireless signals in the air.

Fleming's discovery led an American inventor, Lee De Forest, to see what would happen if he inserted another plate in a bulb to make a "triode." What did happen brought about a further revolution in communication.

Lee De Forest was a minister's son whose early life was filled with the normal pleasures of boyhood and with an enormous curiosity about every kind of machinery. When he wasn't in school or playing baseball or swimming or fishing, he was reading books and magazines about engines and inventions, and when he became a student at Yale University he began to invent gadgets of his own.

Leaving Yale, De Forest worked for a telegraph company in 1900 and designed certain new transmitters, but in 1901 he left to go into business for himself in the production and sale of a new kind of wireless transmitter he had created. The transmitter developed so many "bugs" that the business failed.

The next year, 1902, De Forest and a stock promoter named Abraham White founded the DeForest Wireless Telegraph Company, which was given orders for equipment by the War and Navy Departments. The company probably could have succeeded if its directors had not double-crossed De Forest with underhanded deals which gobbled up the finances, and a few years later when De Forest discovered the cheating he left to form his own De Forest Radio Telephone Company.

In 1903 De Forest made one of the greatest discoveries of his career. In making studies of gases as conductors of electricity, he made a diode using a carbon filament and a platinum (instead of copper) plate in the bulb. He believed the gases created inside the bulb would be ionized (form electrically charged particles) and thus make a more efficient wave detector. To build up the ionizing process he surrounded the bulb with a piece of tin foil which was connected to his antenna. Actually this tin foil represented a third electrode.

The experiment showed that he was on the right track, but he decided that the wave detection would be better if he put the third electrode *inside* the bulb. Instead of the tin foil, he first used a perforated piece of platinum, but he replaced this with a strip of wire "bent back and forth" in zigzag fashion and called a "grid."

The wire grid exceeded even De Forest's expectations. Not only did it detect radio signals, but it also amplified them, which meant that several of the bulbs would be able to capture a very weak wave and transform it into a strong one.

De Forest called his invention an "audion," but it was also known as a "triode" because of its three principal parts. Although De Forest continued to experiment, the audion provided the basis for the millions of vacuum tubes later used in radio and television sets the world over, and it made De Forest a wealthy man.

Although another American, Reginald Fessenden, deserves credit for pioneering work in the transmission and receiving of voices and other sounds by radio, Lee De Forest is the inventor who made this miracle of communication practicable.

The progress of peacetime inventions was interrupted in 1914 when Europe became embroiled in a war which brought ruin and death to several nations, and into which the United States in 1917 sent thousands of men and weapons "to make the world safe for Democracy." It was called the World War, but later, when parts of the world became very *unsafe* for democracy, another bigger war was to make it necessary to refer to the 1914 conflict as "World War I."

World War I created an abnormal expansion of American industry. At the outset America maintained her neutrality, and factories hummed night and day to produce military and other supplies for Great Britain and her allies. As a neutral the United States could also sell goods to Britain's enemies, led by Germany, but a British blockade of German shipping, coupled with British trade regulations enforced against American vessels, made it impossible for the Germans to get or carry American-made merchandise.

The Germans set up a "danger zone" around England, theatening to sink all enemy merchant ships that entered it. The United States protested, and President Woodrow Wilson warned that the German government would be held strictly accountable if any American citizens or vessels were attacked. A tragic answer to his warning came on May 7, 1915, when the British liner *Lusitania* was sunk without warning by a German submarine off the Irish coast. Among some 1100 passengers were 128 Americans.

For several months diplomatic notes were exchanged between the United States and German governments. German promises were made but not all were kept, and they were finally withdrawn when, on January 31, 1917, the German government announced that it would sink *all* ships in the war zone, regardless of their country of registry.

This threat hurt the American economy in an unforeseen way. Owners of merchant ships, fearful that their vessels would be sunk, kept them idle at docks. Food, oil and coal piled up in warehouses. Tons of freight were unloaded from freight trains in various cities, and railroad traffic was tied in knots. Americans began to suffer from shortages of food and coal. Factories had no outlets for goods intended for export.

True to the January promise, German U-boats in March, 1917, sank three ships carrying American passengers, and on April 6 the United States issued a formal declaration of war against Germany.

A great deal of money was needed to finance the war. Airplanes were becoming an important military weapon, and airplane factories were producing them rapidly and at substantial costs. The government sold war bonds, war savings certificates and thrift stamps, and imposed new taxes or increased existing ones, such as the income tax. New government agencies created for special wartime activities included the War Industries Board, which controlled American industry, even specifying what materials could or could not be made, or what new products must be manufactured and at what prices.

Thousands of men who were drafted into the armed forces created a serious labor shortage, and the demand for skilled workmen resulted in extra-high pay and higher costs of living.

On November 11, 1918, an armistice ended World War I with victory for the Allies, and the American fighting men came home. Government contracts for weapons and other war supplies were speedily canceled, and the factories which made them suddenly discovered that they had no orders for peacetime goods. No orders, no work. Thousands of employees were discharged, and the returning men in uniform found themselves among the unemployed.

Soon, however, civilians realized that they could buy merchandise that had not been available in wartime. They could cash their war bonds and certificates and spend the money for "luxuries." Factories gradually began to produce peacetime goods again, not only for American customers but also for export to European countries rebuilding their war-torn cities and industries. Employment picked up. Production could not meet the growing demand, so prices zoomed upward.

Farmers, too, were basking in new-found prosperity. Tons of food were needed overseas, and farmers mortgaged their homes and land to get cash for down payments to buy cattle, reapers, tractors and other equipment on the installment plan.

Labor unions sought higher wages and shorter hours and in

1919 ordered millions of their members to go out on strike to force manufacturers to meet their demands. Higher wages meant increased prices, and by 1921 there were loud protests from American families who could no longer afford to buy certain goods. Foreign countries, too, slacked off in buying American merchandise because of its high costs and tariffs. As a result retail stores lost business and money, factory warehouses began to fill up with unsold products, and farmers awoke to the fact that nations overseas were growing foodstuffs of their own or were buying them at lower costs from countries other than the United States.

For many months the country was on an economic downgrade, but by 1924 the government reduced certain tax rates, established a cooperative marketing movement for farmers, paid subsidies to builders of ships and aircraft and took other steps to get the economy rolling uphill once more.

It was at just about this time that a new development in electronic communication had its beginnings. Dr. Vladimir K. Zworykin, a native of Russia who came to the United States just after World War I, became a research scientist for the Westinghouse Electric Corporation. Since 1906 Dr. Zworykin had conducted experiments not only in radio communication, but also aimed at transmitting pictures through the air electronically.

As the result of his knowledge in this field and his research, he developed the "iconoscope," a special vacuum tube designed for picture transmission, and the "kinescope," another kind of tube whose function was to receive and show the images that were broadcast. In 1923 in the presence of several Westinghouse representatives he actually sent through the air a picture of a cross which was reproduced on his kinescope. The television age had begun.

Other inventors also interested in the electronic transmission of pictures included Philo Farnsworth who, at the age of nineteen, designed a successful TV camera and receiver; Dr. Al Rose, who created the "orthicon" tube and who also, with H. B. Law and Paul Weimar, developed the "image orthicon," which is used in modern television cameras to pick up an image and change its lights and shadows into electronic impulses. These whiz through the air, are captured by television receivers in our homes and are reconverted to the lights and shadows that make up our TV programs.

Television was not to enter the industrial scene or the average home for several years after its principles were first tested—but this was not due to any lack of money by the purchasing public.

From 1925 to 1929—the era of bootleggers, "flappers," gangsters and gun molls—the country was again on a prosperity spree. The stock market was hitting new highs and thousands of people who had never before speculated bought and sold stocks "on margin" (part payment) in attempts to get rich quick. Factory owners built new plants to handle the increased business they anticipated. Promoters bought land, often worthless, and sold it at handsome profits (just as others had done years before). The automobile industry was mushrooming, and new cars were being bought on the installment plan along with new houses, furnishings, clothing, jewelry and almost everything else. The aircraft industry was expanding. Radios were going into homes across the land. Prices were going up and up, but money was plentiful and easy to borrow, and millions of Americans seemed to be "rolling in dough." They were mostly unsuspecting Humpty-Dumpties, with gold-plated shells that were already beginning to crack.

CHAPTER 12

Pushbuttons and Portents

In 1928, when President Coolidge was urged to run for a second term, he made a terse and now-famous announcement: "I do not choose to run."

With great fanfare and ballyhoo about the country's unprecedented prosperity the Republicans nominated Herbert Hoover, an engineer who had served as Coolidge's Secretary of Commerce, and he was elected President.

The lessons history teaches are often forgotten. In 1929, as in days long gone, the overexpansion of industry, the speculation in lands, stocks and merchandise, together with high wages and abnormally high prices, rose to a peak that collapsed of its own weight. Borrowers were asked to repay loans but were unable to do so. Merchandise piled up as customers stayed away, so factories began to fire workers. Business in general took a slump, and in October the prices of stocks went down, down, down until they hit rock bottom and the stock market crashed. Millions of speculators and ordinary investors lost fortunes and nest eggs. Hundreds of companies went broke. Scores of banks closed their doors, and the life savings of thousands of families vanished. Factories shut down; jobless men tramped the streets. Prices of food and other goods dropped, but few people had money to buy more than necessities. Many desperate businessmen killed themselves. The country sank into a deep and dark economic depression. Could "all the King's horses" ever put Humpty-Dumpty together again?

In 1932 the voters blamed the Republicans for the financial disaster and voted overwhelmingly for the Democratic presidential nominee, Franklin Delano Roosevelt. "The only thing we have to fear is fear itself," he declared in his inaugural address.

The people demanded action and they got it. Roosevelt declared a "bank holiday" and closed all banks temporarily. Those that proved to be shaky were not reopened. Laws were drafted and eventually enacted to insure bank accounts up to $10,000. An "Agricultural Adjustment Administration" worked to raise farm prices by cutting farm production, thus helping the beleaguered farmers. A National Labor Relations Act was passed, guaranteeing the right of workers to join labor unions or not, and promising protection to those who decided to enter into collective bargaining with their employers. Many new government agencies (WPA, CCC, etc.) were created to put millions of unemployed men to work on conservation, roadbuilding and civic projects. More new laws and new federal agencies to administer them came into being throughout Mr. Roosevelt's first term, which was popularly called "The New Deal."

Across the Atlantic in the early days of the New Deal there were other developments that would have world-wide repercussions. A paperhanger named Adolf Hitler toppled the government of the German Republic in 1933, set himself up as a dictator and began a reign of terror against all Jews. In Italy democratic government had been abolished since 1922 when Benito Mussolini became Italy's totalitarian ruler. His troops stormed into Ethiopia in 1935 as the start of a great conquest. In 1937 Japan invaded the Chinese mainland. In 1938 Hitler took over Austria and part of Czechoslovakia. Poland became a football kicked by Germany and Russia, who divided up that country as boys divide a bag of candy. In 1939 England and France declared war on Germany, and World War II exploded.

The United States declared itself neutral, but sold—and later lent or leased—war supplies to Britain, France and Russia. American neutrality could not last. On December 7, 1941, Japanese bombing planes launched a sneak attack on American warships and land installations at Pearl Harbor, Hawaii, and the next day President Roosevelt asked Congress to declare war against Japan. Italy, Germany, Japan and their satellites thus formed an "Axis" as enemies of the United States, Britain, France, Russia and their allies.

As in 1914–1918, the war gave a giant push to American industry. Shipyards were beehives of activity, building thousands of transports, cargo ships, submarines and other vessels. Millions of men and women were called to serve in the armed forces, and other millions to work in defense industries. Factories producing peacetime goods were promptly converted into war production. Billions of dollars were spent for tanks, artillery, rifles and aircraft. Coal mines and oil wells speeded up their output. Farmers increased crops, and homeowners became small-time farmers by growing backyard "victory gardens." Railroads used all available equipment to haul troops and military supplies. Civilian rationing of food, gasoline, shoes, tires and certain other essential goods became necessary.

Most labor unions cooperated in the defense effort by reducing the number of strikes, but the United Mine Workers chose to walk out of soft coal mines in 1943 and hard coal mines in 1945. The government took over and operated the mines, but the miners won their demands for pay raises and returned to work.

In World War II, as in many earlier conflicts, new inventions were born, new industries established. New discoveries about electricity created a growing field of "electronics." Radar, "walkie-talkie" radios, computers, automatic airplane pilots and other devices came into being, and "electronics" became a designation that applied to a multitude of automatic machines and gadgets.

Electronics helped the Nazis to rain destruction on London with a new and terrifying weapon—a jet-propelled "buzz bomb" launched in Germany and automatically aimed to hit the British capital city. This was an outcome of experiments with rockets by Dr. Robert H. Goddard, an American who pioneered in this field and who launched the first liquid-fuel rocket in 1926. People then called him "Looney" Goddard because he made an insane prediction that rockets would one day reach the moon.

As this is being written, American scientists are discussing plans to rocket American astronauts into space for a landing on the moon's surface. Rocket flights in manned spaceships orbiting the earth have already become almost commonplace.

In May, 1945, the Allies conquered Germany and Italy, but Japan was still in the fight. On July 26 the Allies sent Japan a formal notice of terms upon which they would accept her surrender. On July 27 the Japanese replied that they would continue to fight. On August 6, 1945, a lone American bombing plane flew high above military installations in the Japanese city of Hiroshima and dropped one bomb. It was a bomb unlike any that had ever been used in any war. When it exploded it sent a mushroom-like smoke cloud eight miles high, it killed or injured more than 150,000 of the 300,000 people in the city, and utterly destroyed buildings within a radius of several square miles. The blast affected places as far as 250 miles away.

This was the second atomic bomb ever exploded. The first had been set off secretly on July 16 as a test at Alamogordo Air Base, New Mexico. A third leveled the Japanese city of Nagasaki on August 9, 1945, and on August 17 Japan agreed to surrender unconditionally.

The world had now entered two new ages—the Electronic and the Atomic.

Actually the Atomic Age had been in the making for a long time. In 1803 John Dalton, a chemist and physicist, Quaker son of a poor English weaver, wrote a paper which, according to modern scientists, shows that he was approaching the atomic theory.

Beginning in 1787 and for fifty-six years Dalton made more than 200,000 entries in a diary describing his meteorological observations. In 1803 he wrote, "Why does not water admit its bulk of every kind of gas alike? This question I have duly considered, and though I am not able to satisfy myself completely I am nearly persuaded that the circumstances depends on the weight and number of the ultimate particles of the several gases."

In the same paper he included a table of the weights of atoms of a variety of substances such as water, ammonia and carbon dioxide. In other words, Dalton's theory was that all matter was made up of atoms of different weights which combined according to natural laws, and it was this theory that laid the foundation for modern physics.

Following the discovery of radioactivity in 1896 many scientists began to study the atomic structure of radioactive materials. In the years that followed, two British scientists, Ernest Rutherford and Frederick Soddy, explained that radioactivity resulted from the disintegration of atoms of which radioactive materials were composed and from the emission of tiny high-energy particles. It was Rutherford who showed that a single atom consisted of a series of negatively charged electrons (or beta rays) revolving around a positively charged nucleus or core.

Others established gradually that the nucleus was made up of particles called *protons*, having a positive charge, and *neutrons*, having no charge at all.

In 1905 a twenty-six-year-old German-Swiss scientist and mathematician formulated this equation: $E = mc^2$, theorizing that energy (E) is equal to mass times the square of the speed of light (mc^2). In other words, he believed that mass itself was a form of energy, and he said his theory could be proven by a study of radioactive elements. His name, which became famous the world over, was Albert Einstein.

There were stacks of calendar pages between 1905 and 1938, yet the invisible atom formed a kind of link between the two. In 1938 two German scientists, Otto Hahn and Fritz Strassman, conducting experiments in Berlin, bombarded uranium with neutrons from radium-beryllium and discovered barium in the residue material. Barium's mass was completely different from that of uranium. Its appearance in the experiment was a complete and exciting mystery. How did it get there? The answer—and an account of the work that followed—was described in a 1946 report by Corbin Allardice and Edward Trapnell of the Atomic Energy Commission, and is summarized in the paragraphs ahead.

The two scientists wrote about their findings to a woman physicist, Lise Meitner, who was associated with Niels Bohr at the Nobel Institute in Copenhagen, Denmark. Lise Meitner, an Austrian, had once worked closely with Otto Hahn in Germany and had fled that country to escape the evils of Hitler's Nazi regime.

She believed that the barium had resulted from a fission, or breaking up, of the uranium atom, but when she added the atomic masses that remained she discovered that they did not equal the atomic mass of the uranium. In other words, some of the uranium mass had vanished. How? Where had it gone? There could be only one answer—it had been transformed into energy, just as Einstein had predicted some thirty-three years earlier.

Einstein had fled Germany to escape Nazi persecution and was doing research at Princeton University's Institute for Advanced Studies. In 1939 Niels Bohr went to Princeton to discuss the uranium-barium puzzle. Other physicists learned about the visit and its purpose and set out to make further explorations of their own. One of these scientists was an Italian, Enrico Fermi, of Columbia University.

Fermi met Bohr at a science conference in Washington and they talked about radioactivity and fission. For the first time they saw the possibility of a chain reaction. That is, when a uranium atom was split, or fissioned, more neutrons appeared and would react with other uranium atoms to create more fissions, and this effect would go on and on.

Enrico Fermi and several other scientists began experiments to determine how many neutrons were thrown off by fissioning uranium. At Columbia University in 1941 Fermi and his associates studied ways in which they might design a uranium chain reactor, and as their preliminary plans developed, their project was moved to Chicago in 1942 under supervision of the government's Office of Scientific Research and Development. If theories became realities it would be possible to create an atomic bomb with more destructive power than 20,000 tons of TNT. Accordingly, the work became top-secret and was designated as the "Manhattan Project" under the command of Major General L. R. Groves of the United States Army. The experiments took place in a squash court under the west stands of Stagg Field of the University of Chicago.

After many preliminary tests the scientists prepared a large round pile of graphite bricks and uranium in alternating layers. Three sets of metal control rods, including one automatic safety rod, were inserted in the pile. By withdrawing the rods a chain reaction should begin. By replacing them it should be controlled.

The atomic pile, supervised by Dr. Fermi, was constructed carefully and to exact measurements. On December 2 Fermi and his forty-one associates were excited and anxious as preparations began to withdraw the control rods. The first rods were pulled out at 9:45 A.M. by Dr. Fermi's direction, and others were withdrawn, little by little, all morning. With each new pull he studied the fission effect on clicking neutron counters outside the pile.

"Take it out another foot," he would say. Then, "Pull it out six inches more." Constantly he manipulated and checked a slide rule in his hands.

The observers were quiet, but there was a tension in the air that they could feel. If the pile became critical and out of control it could blow apart a sizable section of the city of Chicago.

At 11:35 the counter-clicks were so fast they couldn't be counted. A recording pen on a chart zoomed upward, and so did the fears of the witnesses. Suddenly there was a loud slam as one automatic safety control rod thumped back into the pile, halting the fission.

"Let's go to lunch," Fermi said.

They came back at two o'clock and started again to pull out the controls. At 2:50 the rods were withdrawn another foot. At 3:20 they were moved another six inches. Each time there was an increase in activity, but the pile was not yet self-sustaining, and this was what Fermi and the others were waiting for.

At 3:25 P.M. Fermi said, "Pull it out another foot."

The order was carried out. "This will do it," Fermi declared. "Now the pile will become self-sustaining."

A few moments later the counter-clicks became a steady hum. The charting pen moved steadily upward and Fermi smiled. "The reaction is self-sustaining," he said.

At 3:53 P.M. the rods were put back and the clicks and pen came to a stop. The world's first nuclear chain reactor was a success. Man had finally released and controlled the energy of the nucleus of the atom.

One of Fermi's associates, Dr. E. P. Wigner, produced a bottle of Chianti wine and proposed a toast to the experiment's success. Most of the forty-two men present on this historic occasion autographed the label of the bottle, which was evidently the only written record of names of those who participated in the experiment.

What followed is history. The atomic bomb was made and used in 1945. The more powerful hydrogen bomb is a reality.

The first nuclear-powered submarine, the *Nautilus*, pioneered a growing nuclear United States Navy spearheaded by the Polaris fleet and the aircraft carrier *Enterprise*, and led to the construction of the NS (Nuclear Ship) *Savannah*. Atomic reactors created radioactive isotopes which are of immeasurable value in the treatment of disease and are also used to great advantage in both industry and agriculture. Nuclear power plants supplement the use of coal, oil and natural gas in producing electricity.

Neutrons from an atomic reactor have even served as detectives in seeking solutions to ancient mysteries, according to Dr. Glenn T. Seaborg, chairman of the U. S. Atomic Energy Commission.

"For many years questions have been raised about the cause of the death of the Emperor Napoleon I on the island of St. Helena," Dr. Seaborg explained. "Although he was officially reported to have died of cancer, some have interpreted the symptoms of his illness and death as being due to other causes. If we want to think of it in terms of an historical detective story we can say that the *Case of the Imperial Prisoner* has recently been reopened by the discovery of new evidence. Neutron activation analysis has been carried out on a lock of hair reportedly taken from Napoleon's head immediately following his death. The hair contained thirteen times as much arsenic as is normal for human hair. This, added to other symptoms of his final days, has raised an inference that Napoleon may have suffered from arsenic poisoning."

So much for past and present. What's ahead in our atomic future?

Russian scientists have already sent a rocket to the moon, and the United States hopes to land human observers on the lunar surface by 1970. One day there may be nuclear-powered spaceships to carry passengers to the moon and beyond. Nuclear-powered plants may generate electricity in space stations as they now do on earth. Atomic energy may fuel stations built at the bottom of the sea, where men will explore the ocean's mineral riches and other mysteries.

Electronic computers will be housed in portable packages, ready to provide automatic operation of whole industrial plants or to be used in homes to control temperature, figure income taxes, prepare family budgets and do other chores, like the genie of Aladdin's lamp.

World-wide communication, already a reality thanks to man-made satellites orbiting the earth, will be simplified and improved. Three-dimensional images may one day flit across our television screens. New medicines and chemicals, now undreamed of, will cure the incurable and prolong life. Inventions which today would seem miraculous will be commonplace in the years to come.

We are now in what Dr. Seaborg calls "The Scientific Revolution," and no human being can predict accurately what new marvels may be around the bend ahead. At the turn of the twentieth century Thomas Edison said, "We ought to be ashamed to think that invention has been exhausted with the telegraph, telephone, steam engine, dynamo and camera. The next century should go as far beyond 1900 as 1900 is in advance of 1800."

Despite the tremendous advances that have been made since 1733, when John Kay's flying shuttle started the Industrial Revolution, workers today are fighting the relentless advance of automation, just as others before them opposed new mechanical devices (sometimes by smashing them to bits) and for the same reasons—fear of unemployment. Perhaps the foundation for this fear is greater today than it has ever been, and the problem is of vital importance to America's work force and labor organizations.

Ted F. Silvey of the CIO National Headquarters Staff in Washington, D. C., has made some significant observations on the subject of labor and automation.

"Automation is being called a 'second Industrial Revolution,' " he said. "The word *revolution* means a change so sudden and violent that it upsets and disorganizes stable or orderly society. CIO unions can help control automation and its applications so it will make progress possible without disastrous results to workers, in fact be for the benefit of workers and all of society."

Just what is meant by "automation"? Mr. Silvey's explanation appears to be very simple and understandable. "Let's say you're in your car, driving down the road. You come to a curve, you see the curve, and your eyes tell your brain to instruct your hand to turn the wheel. But you can't turn the wheel perfectly to match the curve. You always either overturn or underturn. If you overturn and stay overturned you're going to be off the side of the road into the ditch. If you underturn and stay that way, you're going to go across the white line into the approaching traffic lane. So, as soon as you have turned the wheel and discern that you have overturned or underturned, you make a self-correction—automatically— you don't even think about it. You turn slightly back or slightly forward. This is self-correction, or feedback."

He continued, "Now when that quality is given to a machine—and it's done now by electronics—it is possible for the machine to make a judgment about the work it did, the output, and decide whether it's right or wrong—and if it's wrong, feed back information to the input and correct it instantly. That's what goes on in the petroleum refinery, that's what goes on in a transfer machine, that's what goes on by the new technology in application to production. Taking the manual, muscle skills of a person, adding to them the perceptive senses, putting them together in a mechanism and thereby replacing the skills of a man. This is automation."

As Silvey points out, today's workman sees himself applying his skills to the production of goods made of glass, metal, wood, rubber, plastics or other materials, but the Scientific Revolution has changed this concept. The so-called white collar workers are outnumbering the "blue collar" workers because the former, with technological know-how, work with knowledge rather than with materials. The machine is rapidly replacing the hand and muscle.

One question raised by Mr. Silvey is whether or not the private enterprise system exists mostly to make a profit for the owners or primarily to provide goods and services for people, with private profit as a by-product. His answer to the first part is "Yes," to the second part, "No," and he firmly believes that these answers must be transposed.

Another question is, "Does automation cause unemployment?" Of course it does, but it also creates new jobs and opportunities for people who are properly trained to step into them. New educational and retraining programs are already in progress to prepare displaced workers for new roles in industry and to teach the younger generation how and where to find its way through the automation maze.

Our employment patterns are changing right now. Says Silvey, "More people will have employment in nonprofit and public enterprise jobs. People who will not work in factories will have to find work in all kinds of other occupations and factory workers whose jobs have been destroyed will have to find new work. The problems and their solutions will make life very interesting for the next ten years. And the CIO will be right in there working on these things, not only through collective bargaining, but through political action, legislative work, education, community organization and all the other areas of relationship of members of CIO unions to the society of which we are a democratic part."

The tug-of-war between capital and labor promises to go on and on, and so does this new Industrial Revolution of which we are a part. Perhaps Dr. Seaborg's term, "Scientific Revolution," is more descriptive of the age. From the spinning wheel and hand loom and cotton gin we have come to machines that turn out Rayon, Nylon, Dacron and other man-made fibers superior in many ways to those produced by Nature.

From James Watt's leaky-boiler steam engine we have come to the Atomic Age and the power of atomic energy.

From the steamboat we have come to nuclear-powered ships.

The steam locomotive has given way to the diesel-powered giant.

The early trails and wagon roads are found only in memories and history books, and now our land is webbed by millions of miles of smooth, wide concrete and asphalt highways.

Down these highways speed millions of high-powered automobiles, and above them we hear the roar of jet aircraft, many of which fly faster than the speed of sound.

Guns and bullets are still used in warfare, but they are puny compared to the awful power of A-bombs and H-bombs which could burn our world to a cinder.

The Wright brothers, with their first powered flight of 120 feet, would gaze in awe at fiery, skyscraper-high rockets hurling men in iron capsules into orbit around the earth preparatory to flights to the moon and planets.

Thus the Industrial Revolution that began so long ago has affected your life and mine, and the lives of millions of others throughout the world.

It made possible the employment of millions and consequent higher standards of living.

It enabled farmers to apply mass-production methods to the growing of crops to feed a burgeoning population.

Automobiles, airplanes, railroads and ships made us mobile, helped to unify the nation and broadened our social, political, international and economic horizons.

The telephone, telegraph, radio and television not only tied us closely together in the maintenance of our democracy, but also put us on speaking terms with the peoples of faraway lands. In addition, these media, along with our newspapers, magazines and books serve to keep us informed of the aims and accomplishments of our government, of new ideas and products, of community problems and solutions, and of attitudes and actions of the governments and peoples of other nations of the world.

Our artists, writers and composers have drawn upon our history for their great contributions to our fine and growing cultural treasury.

Thanks to new discoveries in science and medicine the expected life span of a child born today is far greater than it was a hundred years ago; and we have virtually conquered diseases such as smallpox, tuberculosis and poliomyelitis which once killed or crippled thousands. In fact the fight to prolong lives has created new problems concerning the health, activities and futures of the aged.

Reductions in working hours and increases in wages have

provided us with more leisure time, more recreational facilities and more money to spend on pleasure, culture and education.

Our "population explosion" has brought increased problems of housing, education, crime prevention, national defense, governmental controls, taxation, health, unemployment and sectional political and economic interests.

Where trade and industry were once localized, they now affect, and are affected by, the entire world.

Where once "woman's place was in the home," women today make important contributions to the arts and sciences, hold public office and are active in politics, and work at tasks formerly done only by men.

These and other incredible developments in our industrial society since the days of the spinning jenny are unquestionably the launching pads from which man will fire new and even more amazing inventions into—and out of—this world. As to what they may be, we can only guess. As to what they may do, we can hope and pray that they will benefit all mankind. We have come from spinning wheel to spacecraft. We are going from spacecraft to . . . ? You, young man and young lady, are or will be in the vanguard of these wonderful things to come.

What kind of world will you make?

Bibliography

Age of Enterprise, The, by Thomas C. Cochran and William Miller. Macmillan Co., New York, 1942.

Age of Invention, The, by Holland Thompson, (Vol. 37, *The Chronicles of America.*) Yale University Press, New Haven, Conn., 1921.

American Heritage Magazine, Vol. IX, No. 3, April, 1958.

American Science and Invention, by Mitchell Wilson. Simon and Schuster, New York, 1954.

Enterprising Americans, The, by John Chamberlain. Harper & Row, New York. Copyright 1963 by Time, Inc.

Epic of Steel, The, by Douglas Alan Fisher. Harper & Row, New York, 1963.

First Quarter Century of Steam Locomotives in North America, by Smith Hempstone Oliver. Smithsonian Institution, Washington, D. C., 1956.

From Man to Machine, by Agnes Rogers. Little, Brown & Co., Boston, 1941.

God's Gold, by John T. Flynn. Harcourt, Brace & Co., New York, 1932.

Great Inventions, The, by F. B. Wilkie. J. B. Ruth & Co., Philadelphia, 1883.

History of American Manufactures From 1608 to 1860, A, by J. Leander Bishop. Edward Young & Co., Philadelphia, 1868.

History of Mechanical Inventions, A, by Abbott Payson Usher. Harvard University Press, Cambridge, Mass., 1954.

History of Manufactures in the United States, A, (Vol. II) by Victor S. Clark. Carnegie Institution, Washington, D. C., 1928.

History of the Coal Miners of the United States, by Hon. Andrew Roy. Published by the author.

Industrial History of the United States, by Witt Bowden. Adelphi Co., New York, 1930.

Library of Original Sources, The. Ed. by Oliver J. Thatcher. University Research Extension Co., Milwaukee, Wisconsin, 1917.

Life and Times of Major John Mason, The, by Louis B. Mason. G. P. Putnam's Sons, New York, 1935.

Life's Picture History of Western Man. Time, Inc., New York, 1951.

March of the Iron Men, by Roger Burlingame. Charles Scribner's Sons, New York, 1938.

Massachusetts: A Guide to its Places and People. Houghton, Mifflin Co., 1937.

Oil for the World, by Stewart Schackne and N. D'Arcy Drake. Harper & Bros., New York, 1960.

Our First Century, by R. M. Devens. C. A. Nichols & Co., Springfield, Mass., 1878.

Pennsylvania: A Guide to the Keystone State. American Guide Series. Oxford University Press, New York, 1940.

Pioneer America, by Carl W. Drepperd. Doubleday & Co., New York, 1949.

Popular History of American Invention, A, (Vol. I), ed. by Waldeman Kaempffert. Charles Scribner's Sons, New York, 1924.

Selections Illustrating Economic History Since the Seven Years' War. Compiled by Benjamin Rand. John Wilson & Son, Cambridge, Mass., 1892.

Tinkers and Genius, by Edmund Fuller. Hastings House, New York, 1955.

Wonders of the Nineteenth Century, by J. W. Hanson, W. B. Conkey Co., Chicago, 1900.

Yankee Science in the Making, by Dirk J. Struik. Collier Books, New York, 1962.

Index

About the Author

HARRY EDWARD NEAL was born May 4, 1906 in Pittsfield, Massachusetts, but left there in 1925 to work for the Federal government as a stenographer. In 1957 he retired as Assistant Chief of the U. S. Secret Service to devote all of his time to free-lance writing. Before his retirement he wrote magazine articles and short stories which appeared in many national magazines. Today he concentrates on the writing of both juvenile and adult books, though occasionally he produces magazine pieces as well. Mr. and Mrs. Neal make their home in Weston, Connecticut.